FiLOSOP Culture

Cullure

BOARDROOM
EDITION

For information about school-wide professional development, team training, or individual coaching in the application of Loving our Students on Purpose please contact:

- www.godwinconsulting.com.au
- admin@godwinconsulting.com.au

Editor: Allison Slack
Cover Design by Ashley Beck
Interior Design and Layout by Daniel Morales
ISBN: 978-1-7643121-1-0

DEDICATION

This book is dedicated to West End State School, whose leadership and community have not only embraced *Loving Our Students on Purpose* but live it. Your daily practice of connection, joy, and responsibility has transformed these principles from ideas into a culture of love in which your students learn and thrive.

Books

Loving our Students on Purpose
Cultural Architect (coming 2026)

LoSoP Momentum Series

*(Weekly aligned foundational philosophy of
Loving our Students on Purpose)*
Staffroom Edition--book, ebook, or video series available
Future editions coming soon!

LoSoP Culture Series

(Weekly aligned foundational values to build a Culture of Love)
Boardroom Edition
Staffroom Edition
Primary Classroom Edition
Secondary Classroom Edition
Family Room Edition

Podcasts

Loving Our Students on Purpose Journey Podcast
Culture Daily: Education Edition

Resources Available

www.godwinconsulting.com.au
Explore our full range of LoSoP resources designed to bring
connection and joyful responsibility into everyday practice—from
Desk Flips, Printable Poster Collections, and Flash Cards
to Online Courses, Bookmarks, and more.

For bulk purchases email admin@godwinconsulting.com.au

TABLE OF CONTENTS

BUILDING A CULTURE OF LOVE

Welcome to the LoSoP Culture Series: Boardroom Edition

Creating Cultures Where People Feel Beloved,
Chosen, and Cherished

This series is your invitation to create something lasting: a culture of love where every person in your organisation feels beloved, chosen, and cherished. Whether you're leading in a boardroom, a staffroom, a classroom, or your own family room, the principles in this guide will help you build deeper relationships, grow shared responsibility, restore trust when it's been lost, and develop leaders who lead with clarity, compassion, and courage.

The *LoSoP Culture Series* is built on a simple but transformative truth: love changes everything—not the sentimental kind of love, but the kind that shows up with boundaries, grace, and purpose. The kind of love that speaks the truth, makes space for others, and rebuilds what fear and control have damaged.

Across 40 weekly discussions, you'll explore the foundational ideas that shape sustainable, human-centred leadership cultures. Each session focuses on one key principle of connection, drawn from four powerful pillars: *Healthy Relationships, Joyful Responsibility, Genuine Restoration,* and *Leadership Development.*

This series is designed to align across all the environments where culture is formed. The same weekly theme can be used in a boardroom discussion, a staff meeting, a classroom circle, or a family conversation, allowing teams, schools, and families to reflect on the same values at the same time. It's culture-building with shared language, shared purpose, and collective impact.

What Is a Culture of Love?

A culture of love doesn't happen by accident—it's created on purpose. It's built in the everyday leadership choices we make: when we choose connection over control, presence over pressure, and courage over comfort.

This series is shaped by four guiding truths:

1. Our goal is connection.
2. Love is a powerful choice.
3. Fear is the enemy of connection.
4. Building and protecting connection is a learning journey.

These ideas are woven through every leadership conversation, helping you reflect on the culture you currently carry—and intentionally shape the one you want to create.

The Four Pillars of a Culture of Love

Each 10-week block explores one of the four core pillars that sustain a healthy, love-based leadership culture:

- **Healthy Relationships**--where people feel safe, seen, and supported
- **Joyful Responsibility**--where ownership is embraced and encouragement is shared
- **Genuine Restoration**--where mistakes are repaired with integrity and trust is rebuilt
- **Leadership Development**--where leaders are grown, not just appointed

Together, these pillars help leaders create environments that feel human, build momentum, and multiply influence through connection.

How to Use This Series

You can use this resource flexibly across your leadership rhythm—in board meetings, executive check-ins, strategic planning sessions, professional development, mentoring, or personal leadership reflection. Each session includes a clear concept, thoughtful discussion questions, and practical action steps.

It's not about being perfect. It's about being intentional—showing up with honesty, empathy, and a willingness to lead with love.

Why It Matters

In fast-paced, high-pressure environments, it's easy to default to disconnection, reactivity, or control. But you have the power to lead differently—to shape a culture where trust is earned, responsibility is shared, and leadership is relational.

Week by week, this series will guide you in creating a culture that not only delivers results, but also nurtures people, strengthens teams, and leaves a lasting legacy.

This is culture built on love—on purpose.

A NOTE FROM BERNII

Dear Leaders,

Welcome to the *LoSoP Culture Series: Boardroom Edition*—a resource created to support you as you build a culture of love through your leadership.

Leadership is relational at its core. Whether you're guiding an organisation, a team, or a community, the way you treat people becomes the culture you create. It's not just the big moments that shape a workplace—it's the everyday conversations, decisions, and responses that define how people experience connection, safety, and growth.

This series is designed to help you lead with clarity, courage, and compassion. Each session offers space for personal reflection, meaningful dialogue, and practical actions that build trust and deepen your leadership integrity.

You'll be invited to explore what it means to lead relationally—to take ownership of your impact, to restore when disconnection occurs, and to multiply influence by empowering others. These aren't just professional skills. They're deeply human ones. And they form the foundation of workplaces where people feel beloved, chosen, and cherished.

Just like financial plans or operational systems, building a culture of love takes intention and consistency. There will be moments of progress and moments of challenge—both are signs that you're doing the work.

As you embody these principles, your leadership won't just shape your current team—it will ripple outward, raising up others, creating safe spaces for growth, and leaving a legacy far beyond your title or timeframe.

Thank you for leading this way. Thank you for choosing connection over control, restoration over reactivity, and love over fear.

I'm cheering you on—always.

Warmly,
Bernii

HOW TO USE THE LOSOP CULTURE SERIES: BOARDROOM EDITION

The *LoSoP Culture Series: Boardroom Edition* is a practical, flexible resource designed to support executive teams in creating a culture of love—one marked by connection, responsibility, restoration, and leadership that multiplies others.

This series invites leaders to engage in intentional conversations, reflect on their leadership habits, and practise behaviours that build emotionally safe, high-performing organisational cultures where people feel valued, seen, and empowered.

How to Get Started

1. Weekly Sessions

There are 40 weekly sessions in the series. Each one introduces a core leadership principle drawn from one or more of the four culture-building pillars: *Healthy Relationships, Joyful Responsibility, Genuine Restoration,* and *Leadership Development.*

Each session follows the same structure, offering a consistent rhythm for learning, reflection, and action:

- **Learn**—Engage with the key leadership idea for the week, supported by relevant examples to help it land in your day-to-day leadership context.

- **Let's Make It Real**—Read a short story, leadership metaphor, or personal reflection that brings the concept to life.

- **Discuss**—Use the guided conversation prompts to reflect together as a leadership team. This is where culture is shaped—one honest conversation at a time.

- **Do**—Put the learning into practice during the week. Every leader will apply it differently, but each step helps embed the culture you're building.

- **End-of-Week Reflection**—Use this section to pause and check in personally or as a team. Reflect on what worked, what stretched you, and what you noticed.

2. Flexible Timing

These sessions are designed for meaningful but manageable leadership moments:

- Use them in weekly boardroom or executive meetings.
- Start your leadership huddles or 1:1 check-ins with a 10-minute culture focus.
- Integrate them into retreats, professional development, or strategic planning.

Some sessions will spark rich dialogue. Others may lead to deeper reflection or action planning. Adapt each one to suit your team's needs.

3. Adapt for Your Organisation

Feel free to tailor the language, stories, and applications to suit your unique context.

- Newer leaders may need more clarity and support.
- Senior leaders may want deeper questions or strategic applications.
- Cross-functional teams can reflect on how these ideas show up across departments.

This series is designed to flex around your people and your purpose.

4. Create a Culture of Psychological Safety

Before you begin, take time to co-create a group agreement that encourages respectful, honest, and growth-oriented conversations.

As a leadership team, model the very behaviours you want to see in your culture. Leaders facilitating the discussion are encouraged to go first—sharing openly and modelling vulnerability.

Connection grows when leaders lead with integrity.

5. Track Growth

Use the End-of-Week Reflection as a leadership development checkpoint. Encourage leaders to:

- Record personal reflections
- Share insights with a mentor or peer

- Notice and name moments where they put the learning into action

You might also track culture growth patterns across your organisation over time.

6. Integrate with Your Leadership Framework

This series complements:

- Your organisation's core values
- Culture change and strategic alignment work
- Leadership coaching or mentoring models
- Professional development plans
- Behavioural expectations for leaders

Reinforce the weekly themes in your emails, briefings, team planning, or review processes.

7. Celebrate Progress

When leaders practise these behaviours—celebrate it.

Acknowledge moments of connection, responsibility, or courageous restoration.

Celebrating progress builds belief in the culture you're creating.

8. Revisit and Reinforce

Lasting culture change takes time. Some concepts will resonate immediately. Others may need to be repeated or revisited.

Come back to key ideas often. Pause when needed. Let culture development be a rhythm, not a race.

Final Thoughts

This series is more than a leadership tool. It's a framework for building a culture of love—where connection is the priority, restoration is possible, and leadership leaves a legacy.

Thank you for choosing to lead this way. Your daily choices are shaping the emotional climate of your teams and the future of your organisation.

Together, we can create boardrooms, workplaces, and communities where people feel *beloved, chosen, and cherished*—and where leadership is defined by courage, care, and character.

TOP TIP

GET READY WITH A FEELINGS WHEEL

Before you begin the *LoSoP Culture* Series, we recommend printing a large feelings wheel poster and displaying it in your environment. You can find a variety of feelings wheels online by simply googling "Feelings Wheel." Choose one that suits the age group you're working with.

You may observe that topics in this series include a "How do you feel?" question. It's important to focus on our own experiences, rather than asking, "How did that make you feel?" which can unintentionally place the responsibility for feelings outside the person. By asking "How do you feel?", we support each other to take ownership of our own internal emotional experiences.

Encourage participants to move beyond basic labels like *sad, bad, mad,* or *glad,* and instead explore the feelings wheel to identify a more specific emotion. This simple practice helps expand their emotional vocabulary and builds their capacity to express themselves with clarity and confidence––an essential skill for connection, empathy, and self-awareness.

All emotions are good. They exist to signal that action is needed. Sometimes emotions reveal that a boundary has been crossed and invite us to take responsibility for how we protect our future boundaries. At other times they highlight a need that requires attention, or they expose a fear that has been triggered. Emotions can also be a signal that something deserves to be celebrated. Whatever the emotion, it is doing its job of communicating. Our task is to listen well and respond with wisdom.

PART ONE

CULTIVATING HEALTHY RELATIONSHIPS AT EXECUTIVE LEVEL

Leadership starts with connection.

In this first section, we lay the foundations for a healthy leadership culture—one built on trust, respect, and strong relationships. Executive teams set the tone for how people experience belonging, communication, and collaboration in the organisation.

Healthy relationships in leadership don't happen by accident—they happen by design. This section equips leaders to connect deeply, listen actively, and create safe spaces for growth at every level of the organisation.

WEEK 1:

THE POWER OF LISTENING IN LEADERSHIP

"The most basic and powerful way to connect to another person is to listen. Just listen." —Rachel Naomi Remen

Learn

In executive leadership, listening is not a soft skill—it's a strategic advantage. Leaders who truly listen create environments of trust, psychological safety, and innovation.

Listening is more than hearing words. It's about being fully present— suspending your assumptions, agenda, or solutions to understand the speaker's perspective.

In fast-paced executive spaces, the pressure to provide answers can drown out the discipline of listening. But the most influential leaders listen first and lead second.

Great leaders don't listen to reply. They listen to understand, and in doing so, they unlock creativity, solve complex problems collaboratively, and nurture loyalty.

Consider

Imagine an executive team where the CEO dominates every conversation. Team members hold back ideas, disengage, or avoid raising concerns because they know their voice isn't truly valued.

Now contrast that with a leader who pauses, listens deeply, asks clarifying questions, and genuinely considers input before responding.

Which culture would attract and retain top talent? Which leader multiplies others?

Listening sets the tone for how people experience your leadership.

Let's Make It Real

Share a personal story of a leader who impacted you deeply because they listened well. How did that moment shape your trust in them? Or reflect on a time when poor listening damaged trust or connection in a team you were part of.

(Invite any executive in the room to share a story to model vulnerability and authenticity.)

Discuss

Choose 2-3 of these questions for your boardroom or executive team discussion.

- What does good listening look like for us in this room?
- Where do we tend to listen to reply or defend, rather than to understand?
- How would deeper listening change the way we lead our teams?
- What gets in the way of listening well in fast-paced, high-pressure environments?
- What is one habit or behaviour we could adopt to elevate our listening culture?

Do

This week, commit to a deliberate listening practice:

"In every 1:1 or team conversation this week, I will ask one more clarifying question before I respond or solve."

Examples of clarifying questions:

- "Tell me more about that…"
- "What's most important to you in this?"
- "What do you need from me right now—advice, support, or just space to process?"

Notice the shift in your conversations. Notice how people open up differently when they feel heard.

End-of-Week Reflection

Personal Leadership Check-In:

- How did my listening impact the quality of my conversations this week?

- Where did I notice myself defaulting to problem-solving over presence?
- What feedback have I received about how I listen as a leader?
- What will I do differently next week to create a culture of trust through listening?

WEEK 2:

GIVING AND RECEIVING FEEDBACK AS A CULTURE DRIVER

"Feedback is the breakfast of champions." —Rick Tate

Learn

Feedback is one of the most powerful leadership tools—not just for performance, but for building trust, shaping culture, and multiplying leaders.

In healthy leadership cultures, feedback flows up, down, and across the organisation. It's timely, specific, and framed for growth—not criticism.

Feedback is not about catching people out. It's about creating clarity, aligning values, and unlocking potential.

Great leaders give feedback with courage and kindness, and they invite feedback with humility and curiosity.

How feedback flows in your boardroom will be how feedback flows in your organisation.

Consider

Imagine a boardroom where feedback is avoided or softened to the point of being unhelpful. Issues fester. Growth stalls. The culture becomes one of politeness over progress.

Now picture a boardroom where feedback is normalised, expected, and safe. Leaders give feedback that is specific, clear, and actionable. They ask for feedback regularly and model receiving it without defensiveness.

One culture stays stuck. The other grows rapidly.

Which one describes your leadership environment?

Let's Make It Real

Share a story of the best piece of feedback you've ever received. What did it unlock for you?

Or reflect on a time you avoided giving feedback. What was the cost to the person, the relationship, or the culture?

Invite any executive to share an example where feedback shaped them personally or professionally.

Discuss

Choose 2-3 of these questions for group discussion.

- What is the feedback culture like in this team?

- What are we modelling about giving and receiving feedback?

- What's harder for me—giving feedback or receiving it? Why?

- What's one thing we could do to normalise healthy feedback in our leadership environment?

- How do we create feedback processes that build people, not break them?

Do

This week, practise both giving and receiving feedback.

1. Identify one person you need to give feedback to and frame it for growth:
   - Be specific.
   - Be kind.
   - Be clear.
   - Be helpful.

2. Ask for feedback from someone you lead or work alongside. Use this language:
   "I'm working on improving how I lead. What's one thing I could do more of or less of that would help me serve this team better?"

Receive their feedback with gratitude. No defensiveness. Just curiosity.

End-of-Week Reflection

Personal Leadership Check-In:

- Who did I give feedback to this week, and how was it received?
- How did I respond to feedback I received?
- What did this feedback process reveal about our current culture?
- What is one leadership habit I will practise to help create a feedback-rich culture going forward?

WEEK 3:

EMPATHY––THE LEADERSHIP ADVANTAGE

"Leadership is not about being in charge. It is about taking care of those in your charge." —Simon Sinek

Learn

Empathy is not a weakness in leadership—it's a competitive advantage.

Empathy is the skill of seeing from another's perspective. It's the ability to pause, notice, and understand what people are experiencing beneath the surface of performance.

In boardrooms, empathy helps leaders navigate complexity, change, and conflict without losing people in the process.

Empathy doesn't remove accountability—it humanises it.

Empathy says: "I see you. I hear you. And I still believe you are capable and responsible."

This is what earns the trust and loyalty that strategy alone cannot buy.

Consider

Imagine a boardroom where empathy is absent. Metrics matter more than people. Deadlines outweigh well-being. Staff burnout rises. Trust declines.

Now picture a leadership culture where empathy is present in every conversation—not as indulgence, but as wisdom.

Leaders notice stress early.

They ask powerful human questions:

"What's going on for you right now?"

"What do you need to be at your best?"

They pair empathy with expectation.

Empathy doesn't remove hard conversations—it makes them safe enough to have.

Let's Make It Real

Share a story of a time when someone led you with empathy. How did it change your engagement or loyalty?

Alternatively, reflect on a time when empathy was absent in leadership. What did it cost?

Invite the boardroom to share their reflections.

Discuss

Choose 2-3 questions for your team discussion.

- How would our people describe the empathy level of this leadership team?
- What happens in our culture when empathy is absent?
- Where have we mistaken empathy for weakness?
- How do we practise empathy while maintaining high expectations?
- What do we need to get better at noticing in our teams?

Do

This week, practise "Empathy + Expectation" in every leadership interaction.

Step 1: Pause to Notice.

What's going on for this person beneath the behaviour or performance?

Step 2: Ask One Empathy Question.

"What's going on for you right now?"

"What do you need from me?"

Step 3: Reset Expectation.

"I hear you. I also know you are capable of working through this. Let's talk about what's next."

Empathy connects. Expectation empowers.

End-of-Week Reflection

Personal Leadership Check-In:

- Where did I practise empathy well this week?
- How did empathy change the tone or direction of a conversation?
- Where do I need to slow down and notice more as a leader?
- What is one habit I will build to become a more empathetic and empowering leader?

WEEK 4:

COMMUNICATING WITH KINDNESS & INFLUENCE

"People will forget what you said, people will forget what you did, but people will never forget how you made them feel."
—Maya Angelou

Learn

The most influential leaders communicate with clarity and kindness.

Kindness in leadership is not about being "nice" to avoid hard things—it's about delivering truth in a way people can receive.

Kindness protects connection. Clarity protects expectations. Influence happens when both are present.

Boardroom communication sets the tone for every layer of an organisation. If communication is vague, reactive, or careless at the top, it echoes throughout the culture.

When leaders speak with kindness and clarity, trust accelerates, conflict reduces, and people perform better because they know where they stand.

Consider

Imagine an executive team where communication is sharp, rushed, or emotionally reactive. People withdraw. Energy drops. Fear rises.

Now imagine a leadership culture where communication is intentional, calm, and kind, even in pressure moments.

Clarity is delivered without harshness. Expectations are set without fear. Feedback is framed in a way that honours dignity.

This doesn't slow down business—it speeds up trust.

Let's Make It Real

Share a story of a time when someone communicated hard truth to you with kindness. How did it shape your trust or growth?

Or share a moment when careless communication damaged a team or culture. What was the long-term cost?

Invite your executives to reflect and share.

Discuss

Choose 2-3 of these for team discussion.

- What communication habits do we model in this boardroom?

- Where does our communication lean—too much clarity with not enough kindness? Or kindness without clarity?
- How do we want people to feel after interactions with us?
- What stories are our words writing about our culture?
- What language habits do we need to change to lead with greater influence?

Do

This week, practise a new communication habit:

Before I speak, I will ask myself:

"Will this build trust?"

"Is this clear?"

"Is this kind?"

Consider introducing a "Cultural Check-In" for your team:

In meetings, pause and ask:

"Is there anything I said today that didn't land how I intended?"

"Is there anything I need to clarify or own?"

This models courageous, influential communication.

End-of-Week Reflection

Personal Leadership Check-In:

- Where did my words build trust this week?

- Where did I default to clarity without kindness—or kindness without clarity?
- What feedback have I received about how I communicate?
- What communication habit do I need to practise next week to increase my influence?

WEEK 5:

SOLVING COMPLEX PROBLEMS COLLABORATIVELY

"If you want to go fast, go alone. If you want to go far, go together." —African Proverb

Learn

The problems facing organisations today are rarely solved by a single leader—they require collaboration.

Collaboration is not about consensus. It's about creating an environment where diverse thinking is welcomed, conflict is safe, and responsibility is shared.

In executive leadership, the way you solve problems is often more important than how quickly you solve them.

Poor problem-solving cultures are reactive, siloed, and personality-driven. Collaborative problem-solving cultures are curious, courageous, and collective.

Complexity requires collaboration—because nobody sees the whole picture alone.

Consider

Imagine a boardroom where problem-solving is dominated by the loudest voice or most senior title. Ideas are shut down. Risk is avoided. People stay silent. The best solutions are missed.

Now imagine a boardroom where complex problems are approached with curiosity, humility, and a willingness to listen across departments, roles, and perspectives.

Collaborative leadership is not slower—it prevents costly mistakes.

It builds ownership at every level because people feel part of the solution, not just recipients of decisions.

Let's Make It Real

Share a story of a time when collaboration led to a breakthrough in your leadership. Who contributed? What perspective changed the outcome?

Alternatively, reflect on a time when problem-solving went badly because collaboration was absent. What did it cost?

Invite executives to share reflections.

Discuss

Choose 2-3 of these for discussion.

- How would our teams describe the way we solve problems together?
- Where does collaboration break down in our culture?
- Who do we need to involve earlier in our decision-making processes?
- How can we create safer spaces for disagreement and debate?
- What behaviours build or break collaborative trust here?

Do

This week, practise Collaborative Problem-Solving Leadership.

In your next complex challenge:

- Invite someone into the conversation who sees from a different vantage point.
- Ask: *"Who else needs to speak into this before we decide?"*
- Frame the problem not as *"How do I fix this?"* but *"How do we solve this together?"*

Notice how perspectives widen and ownership grows.

End-of-Week Reflection

Personal Leadership Check-In:

- Where did I model collaborative problem-solving well this week?

- Where did I default to solo decision-making or assumption?
- Who did I invite to the table who isn't normally there?
- What will I change about how I lead in complex challenges going forward?

WEEK 6:

RESPECT AS A LEADERSHIP DISCIPLINE

"When people respect you as a person, they admire you. When they respect you as a friend, they love you. When they respect you as a leader, they follow you." —John C. Maxwell

Learn

Respect is not earned by position—it's built by behaviour.

In leadership, respect is a daily discipline. It shows up in how we speak, how we listen, how we challenge, and how we follow through.

In the boardroom, respect sets the standard for how people will treat each other throughout the organisation.

It's easy to respect those we like, those we agree with, or those who perform well.

Leadership respect is measured in how we treat:

- The frustrated employee
- The underperformer
- The difficult conversation
- The team who will never "return the favour"

Respect is not passive politeness—it's active commitment to dignity.

Consider

Imagine a culture where respect is conditional, given only when people meet expectations or perform.

Trust declines. Psychological safety erodes. Teams protect themselves instead of collaborating.

Now picture a culture where respect is non-negotiable, regardless of performance, disagreement, or rank.

Respect isn't about excusing poor behaviour—it's about modelling the behaviour you want to multiply.

Leaders who respect people create people who respect the culture.

Let's Make It Real

Share a story of a leader who demonstrated respect in a challenging moment. How did their behaviour impact you or the team?

Alternatively, reflect on a time when respect was absent in leadership. What was the impact on connection, morale, or performance?

Invite the boardroom to share stories or reflections.

Discuss

Choose 2-3 of these for discussion.

- How do we define respect in this leadership team?
- Where is respect tested most in our culture?
- Where might people experience us as dismissive or disconnected?
- What does it look like to lead with respect even in conflict or correction?
- How do we protect a culture of respect when under pressure?

Do

This week, practise Respect as a Leadership Discipline.

- Notice who you are tempted to dismiss, interrupt, or overlook.
- Practise slowing down and demonstrating intentional respect, especially in challenge, correction, or disagreement.
- Model curiosity over judgement. Say: *"Help me understand your perspective."*

Respect isn't agreement — it's how you carry disagreement.

End-of-Week Reflection

Personal Leadership Check-In:

- Where did I practise respect well this week—especially when it was hard?

- Where did I slip into reactive, dismissive, or positional leadership?

- How would my team describe how I show respect?

- What is one respect habit I need to build into my leadership practice next week?

WEEK 7:

BETTER TOGETHER—BUILDING COHESIVE EXECUTIVE TEAMS

"None of us is as smart as all of us." —Ken Blanchard

Learn

High-performing executive teams are built, not born.

Healthy teams don't happen by accident. They are the result of shared trust, robust communication, clear expectations, and mutual account-ability.

In executive leadership, your team culture either accelerates strategy or sabotages it.

Cohesive leadership teams:

- Know how to disagree well.

- Speak directly and kindly.

- Assume positive intent.

- Align around shared purpose, not personal agenda.

Poorly functioning teams create fear, competition, silos, and mistrust—even if everyone is talented.

Talent doesn't build culture. Trust does.

Consider

Imagine an executive team where decisions are made outside the room, alliances form in whispers, and silence replaces honesty.

Now picture a team where differences are welcomed, challenges are safe, and alignment is fought for, not assumed.

Cohesive teams lead cultures of connection, clarity, and high performance.

If it's dysfunctional in the boardroom, it will be dysfunctional in the organisation.

Let's Make It Real

Share a story of the best leadership team you've been part of. What made it different? What habits or behaviours set it apart?

Alternatively, reflect on a time when a leadership team you were part of fractured. What caused disconnection or distrust?

Invite reflection and discussion around what healthy teams require.

Discuss

Choose 2-3 of these for team discussion.

- What are we like as a leadership team when things are hard?
- Where do we fall into patterns of avoidance, assumption, or unhealthy silence?
- What behaviours build trust here—and what behaviours break it?
- How do we want people in our organisation to describe us as a team?
- What will it take for us to be "better together"?

Do

This week, practise one behaviour that builds a cohesive team.

- Address a small tension before it grows.
- Give visible encouragement or recognition to a teammate.
- Ask for feedback on how you show up in the team.
- Practise disagreeing with curiosity, not combat.

Say: *"Can you help me understand your thinking on that?"*

This creates space for difference without division.

End-of-Week Reflection

Personal Leadership Check-In:

- Where did I contribute to greater trust and connection in our team this week?

- Where did I notice patterns that disconnect or divide us?

- How would this team describe my impact—do I build or erode cohesion?

- What do I need to keep practising to help us lead better together?

WEEK 8:

BUILDING TRUST THAT SCALES

"Trust doesn't mean that you trust that someone won't screw up—it means you trust them when they do screw up."
—Ed Catmull

Learn

Trust is the currency of every great leadership team. It's also the slowest thing to build and the fastest thing to break.

In executive leadership, scalable trust means building systems and behaviours where people know:

- They are safe to be honest.
- They are responsible for their actions.
- They can fail forward without fear.

Trust is not built through perfection—it's built through consistent repair.

Trust that scales is trust that survives mistakes, pressure, growth, and change.

It's not a one-time achievement—it's a lifelong leadership discipline.

Consider

Imagine an organisation where trust is conditional based on performance, agreement, or appearance.

People hide problems. Teams protect themselves. Mistakes are buried rather than owned.

Now imagine a culture where trust is reinforced through ownership, honesty, and repair.

People say: *"Here's what happened. Here's how I'm owning it. Here's how I'll fix it."*

This is what creates a resilient, scalable trust culture.

Let's Make It Real

Share a story of a time when you saw trust deepen in a leadership relationship—not because someone was perfect, but because they repaired well.

Alternatively, reflect on a moment when trust was broken in leadership. What were the behaviours that restored it or damaged it further?

Invite the boardroom to share reflections.

Discuss

Choose 2-3 of these for discussion.

- How is trust built and rebuilt in this team?
- Where do we need to practise repair more intentionally?
- What behaviours break trust fastest in our culture?
- What stories would our people tell about trust in this organisation?
- What does it mean to lead with trust that scales, especially when mistakes happen?

Do

This week, practise building scalable trust.

Look for one moment where trust is tested, and lean into repair.

Say:

"Here's what I own in this."

"Here's what I'll do next."

Trust grows most in the moments you want to avoid.

Model repair publicly when appropriate—this teaches your teams how to do the same.

End-of-Week Reflection

Personal Leadership Check-In:

- Where did I build or repair trust this week?
- Where did I avoid a trust-building moment?
- How would my team describe my trust leadership?
- What behaviours do I need to reinforce to lead a scalable trust culture?

WEEK 9:

BALANCING THE RESPONSIBILITY AND RELATIONSHIP MATRIX

"You can't have a strong relationship without taking responsibility for your words and actions." —Gary Chapman

Learn

Healthy leadership holds two tensions in balance—Responsibility and Relationship.

Responsibility without Relationship feels transactional, cold, or authoritarian.

Relationship without Responsibility feels chaotic, unclear, or permissive.

Powerful leaders know both matter.

Responsibility is about accountability, clarity, and ownership.

Relationship is about connection, empathy, and trust.

At scale, organisations drift when leaders prioritise one over the other.

Great leadership cultures align both.

We say:

"I care about you deeply—and I expect you to take ownership of your behaviour."

This balance creates organisations that are both deeply human and highly responsible.

Consider

Imagine a boardroom that swings toward heavy responsibility. Metrics matter more than people. Fear rises. Innovation shrinks.

Now imagine a boardroom that swings toward relationship only. Everyone feels cared for but expectations are loose. Accountability weakens.

Balanced leadership is not about the middle ground—it's about strength in both.

Responsibility fuels growth. Relationship fuels connection. Together they sustain culture.

Let's Make It Real

Share a story of a time when you experienced a leader balancing responsibility and relationship well. What was the impact on you or the organisation?

Alternatively, reflect on a time when one of these was missing. What happened to trust, culture, or results?

Invite reflection and sharing.

Discuss

Choose 2-3 of these for your team discussion.

- Where do we as a team tend to drift--towards responsibility without relationship, or relationship without responsibility?
- What behaviours have we normalised that signal imbalance?
- How do we want people in our organisation to experience both care and accountability from us?
- What structures or rhythms could help us keep this balance visible?
- Where do we need to re-align our leadership practice this term?

Do

This week, practise Balancing Responsibility and Relationship.

Choose one conversation where you need to:

- Connect personally first—ask, *"How are you really doing?"*
- Then call up responsibility—say, *"Here's what I need from you moving forward."*

Relationship opens the heart. Responsibility moves the hand.

Both together change culture.

End-of-Week Reflection

Personal Leadership Check-In:

- Where did I balance responsibility and relationship well this week?
- Where did I avoid one or favour the other?
- How did my team respond when I led with both?
- What do I need to keep practising to lead a culture of both high connection and high responsibility?

WEEK 10:

EMPOWERING OTHERS TO LEAD USING THE EMPOWERMENT MODEL

"A friend is someone who gives you total freedom to be yourself." —Jim Morrison

Learn

Empowering leadership is not about rescuing people—it's about equipping them.

The Empowerment Model gives leaders a practical tool for raising others into responsibility, ownership, and confidence.

Empowerment is not: *"Let me fix this for you."*

Empowerment is: *"I believe you have what it takes to solve this."*

In executive leadership, this mindset develops capable leaders at every level, reducing dependency and increasing ownership.

Empowerment cultures multiply leaders, not followers.

The Empowerment Model—6 Leadership Steps

1. Empathy: "That sounds tough."
   (Acknowledge their challenge without taking ownership of it.)

2. Empower: "What are you going to do?"
   (Hand responsibility back to them.)

3. Explore: "What have you tried already?"
   (Invite reflection and learning.)

4. Educate: "I have some ideas if you'd like them."
   (Offer wisdom without control.)

5. Expect: "What will you do next?"
   (Create clear ownership of next steps.)

6. Encourage: "Let me know how it goes."
   (Stay connected but not responsible for the outcome.)

This simple framework raises up powerful people and breaks cycles of dependency.

Consider

Imagine a culture where every problem is escalated upwards—where leaders carry not only their own responsibilities but everyone else's.

Now imagine a culture where leaders are taught, equipped, and expected to own their challenges—supported, but not rescued.

Empowerment doesn't lighten the load—it distributes it wisely.

Empowered people own their results.

Let's Make It Real

Share a story of a time when you experienced empowering leadership—where someone didn't solve the problem for you but believed in your capacity to lead.

Alternatively, reflect on a time when rescuing leadership stunted growth or created unhealthy dependency.

Invite reflections from the room.

Discuss

Choose 2-3 of these for team discussion.

- Where in our leadership culture do we default to rescuing over empowering?
- What message does rescuing send to our teams?
- How do we build the skill and mindset of empowerment into our daily leadership practice?
- Where do we need to get better at handing responsibility back to others?
- What would shift in our culture if we led this way consistently?

Do

This week, practise the Empowerment Model in one key conversation.

When someone brings a problem to you:

- Empathise first.
- Ask: *"What are you going to do?"*

- Explore what they've tried.
- Offer ideas if invited.
- Expect ownership of next steps.
- Encourage follow-through.

Notice the shift in responsibility and confidence.

End-of-Week Reflection

Personal Leadership Check-In:

- Where did I practise empowerment well this week?
- Where did I rescue instead of equip?
- How did people respond when I handed responsibility back?
- What do I need to keep practising to become an empowering leader who multiplies others?

SECTION TWO

LEADING WITH JOYFUL RESPONSIBILITY

Responsibility isn't a burden—it's a privilege.

This section shifts the leadership mindset from control or obligation into powerful ownership. Joyful responsibility means leaders own their behaviour, their growth, and their impact with energy, integrity, and care.

When responsibility is carried joyfully, accountability flows naturally. People step up—not because they have to, but because they want to. This section strengthens executive capacity for leading with clarity, ownership, and resilience.

WEEK 11:

OWNING YOUR ACTIONS AND ORGANISATIONAL IMPACT

*"Responsibility equals accountability equals ownership.
And a sense of ownership is the most powerful weapon a team
or organization can have."* —Pat Summitt

Learn

Ownership is one of the clearest indicators of powerful leadership.

Powerful leaders don't blame others. They don't avoid responsibility. They don't wait for permission to act.

Ownership says: *"I am responsible for my actions, my influence, and my impact regardless of circumstance."*

In the boardroom, ownership transforms culture. It creates trust, speeds decision-making, and builds credibility.

A culture of ownership is not created by policies—it's modelled by behaviour.

Leaders who own their part invite others to do the same.

Leaders who avoid responsibility create cultures of blame and avoidance.

Consider

Imagine a leadership team where mistakes are hidden, responsibility is avoided, and blame is passed around the table.

Now imagine a team where leaders own their actions quickly and clearly.

They say:

"This didn't go as planned. Here's what I own, here's what I've learned, and here's what I'll do differently."

That behaviour sets the standard.

Ownership isn't about being perfect—it's about being accountable.

Let's Make It Real

Share a story of a time when you saw courageous ownership in leadership. How did it build trust or shift culture?

Alternatively, reflect on a moment where avoidance or blame created unnecessary damage.

Invite reflection and sharing.

Discuss

Choose 2-3 of these for team discussion.

- How would people in our organisation describe our ownership culture?
- Where do we as a leadership team need to model ownership more intentionally?
- What behaviours do we need to eliminate that undermine ownership?
- How do we create safe environments where owning mistakes is normalised?
- What does personal responsibility look like at the executive level?

Do

This week, practise radical ownership.

Look for a moment where you could:

- Own a mistake.
- Own your part of a difficult situation.
- Own your impact—even if unintended.

Model the language of ownership:

"Here's what I own."

"Here's what I've learned."

"Here's what I'll do next."

This will shift culture faster than any policy.

End-of-Week Reflection

Personal Leadership Check-In:

- Where did I practise courageous ownership this week?
- Where did I notice patterns of avoidance or blame in myself or others?
- How would my team describe my ownership leadership?
- What do I need to keep practising to lead a culture of ownership at every level?

WEEK 12:

POWERFUL LEADERS CREATE POWERFUL CULTURES

"Powerful people do not try to control other people.
They know it doesn't work, and that it's not their job.
Their job is to control themselves." —Danny Silk

Learn

Leadership power is not control—it's responsibility.

In every organisation, there are three ways people relate to power:

1. Powerless + Powerless = Controlling
   When both parties feel powerless, they attempt to control each other to feel safe. Fear drives this behaviour.

2. Powerless + Powerful = Codependent
   One person takes all the responsibility, while the other becomes dependent and avoids ownership.

3. Powerful + Powerful = Freedom
   Both parties take responsibility for themselves. They collaborate, honour boundaries, and lead with mutual respect.

Powerful leaders take responsibility for themselves—not for managing or controlling others.

Culture shifts when leaders stop over-functioning for their people and start empowering them.

Consider

Imagine a leadership team where power is used to control outcomes, minimise risk, or avoid discomfort.

Teams stop thinking for themselves. Creativity dies. Dependency rises.

Now picture a leadership culture where every leader is responsible for their own actions, mindset, and choices—and expects the same from others.

This creates freedom, trust, and high accountability.

Powerful leadership is not about managing people—it's about managing yourself.

Let's Make It Real

Share a story of a time when you led powerfully by taking responsibility for yourself—even when it would have been easier to control or rescue someone else.

Alternatively, reflect on a time when a culture of control stifled growth or created frustration.

Invite the boardroom to reflect on where they see these patterns.

Discuss

Choose 2-3 of these for discussion.

- Where do we as a team drift toward control instead of responsibility?
- Where have we taken responsibility for things that aren't ours to carry?
- What would shift in our culture if everyone practised powerful leadership?
- How do we want power to be experienced in this organisation?
- What is the cost of codependency in leadership teams?

Do

This week, practise being a Powerful Leader.

- Notice where you're tempted to control or over-function for others.
- Instead, hand responsibility back:
  "That's a great question. What do you think you should do?"
  "How will you take ownership of this?"

Powerful leaders grow powerful people.

End-of-Week Reflection

Personal Leadership Check-In:

- Where did I practise powerful leadership this week?
- Where did I notice controlling or codependent patterns in myself or others?
- How did people respond when I handed back responsibility?
- What do I need to keep practising to lead from power, not control?

WEEK 13:

CHOOSING LOVE OVER FEAR IN ORGANISATIONAL DECISIONS

"There are only two emotions: love and fear. All positive emotions come from love, all negative emotions from fear."
—Elisabeth Kübler-Ross

Learn

Fear and love are at the heart of every leadership decision.

Fear drives self-protection, control, and disconnection.

Love drives connection, trust, and freedom.

Fear in leadership sounds like:

- "If I don't control this, I'll lose respect."
- "If I don't fix this, I'll be blamed."

- "If I'm vulnerable, I'll be seen as weak."

Love in leadership says:

- "I can set boundaries without control."
- "I can trust people to grow through challenge."
- "I can lead with vulnerability and strength."

Fear builds walls. Love builds bridges.

Fear disconnects people. Love connects them.

Leadership is a series of daily choices—fear or love.

Consider

Imagine a leadership culture where fear drives behaviour.

- Fear of failure.
- Fear of transparency.
- Fear of feedback.
- Fear of being wrong.

Now imagine a culture led by love:

- Clear expectations with kindness.
- Feedback framed for growth.
- Boundaries with respect.
- Ownership with grace.

Love is not weakness—it's the strongest force for connection and growth.

Let's Make It Real

Share a story of a time when fear shaped your leadership. What was the cost?

Alternatively, reflect on a moment when you led with love. What was the impact on people, culture, or results?

Invite the team to reflect on how fear or love shows up in their leadership.

Discuss

Choose 2-3 of these for discussion.

- Where does fear show up most in our leadership decisions?
- How would our people describe our leadership culture—fear-based or love-based?
- What behaviours create fear here?
- What would it look like to lead more consistently with love?
- Where do we need to dismantle fear-based patterns in our leadership culture?

Do

This week, practise choosing love over fear in one key leadership interaction.

Ask yourself:

- Am I leading from fear or love right now?
- Am I protecting myself or empowering someone else?

- Am I controlling or trusting?

Choose connection. Choose grace. Choose strength with kindness.

End-of-Week Reflection

Personal Leadership Check-In:

- Where did I notice fear driving my leadership this week?
- Where did I choose love instead—and what was the result?
- How did people respond when I led with love over fear?
- What do I need to keep practising to build a love-based leadership culture?

WEEK 14:

FREEDOM THROUGH BOUNDARIES—SETTING EXECUTIVE LIMITS

"Boundaries define us. They define what is me and what is not me. A boundary shows me where I end and someone else begins, leading me to a sense of ownership." —Dr. John Townsend and Dr. Henry Cloud

Learn

Healthy boundaries are a leadership essential, not a luxury.

Boundaries protect what matters most:

- Your energy.
- Your values.
- Your relationships.
- Your integrity.

Boundaries are not about control—they are about clarity.

Executive leaders without boundaries drift into:

- Overload.
- Resentment.
- Burnout.
- Disconnection.

Boundaries create freedom—for yourself and for others.

In high-performing cultures, clear boundaries release people to thrive, own their role, and lead themselves.

Consider

Imagine a leadership team where boundaries are unclear.

People over-function for each other. Work bleeds into every part of life. Roles are confused. Expectations are unspoken.

Now imagine a leadership team where boundaries are clear.

Expectations are named. Work rhythms are sustainable. Respect is practised. People are free to own their space.

Boundaries clarify responsibility and foster trust.

Let's Make It Real

Share a story of a boundary you've set in leadership that protected something important—your well-being, your family, or your values.

Alternatively, reflect on a time when a lack of boundaries created frustration, exhaustion, or relational damage.

Invite reflection and sharing.

Discuss

Choose 2-3 of these for team discussion.

- What boundaries do we model in this leadership team?
- Where are our boundaries unclear or inconsistent?
- What do our current boundaries say about what we value?
- How do we lead sustainable, healthy rhythms in our leadership culture?
- What boundaries do we need to establish or protect moving forward?

Do

This week, practise setting or protecting one healthy boundary.

Consider:

- Calendar boundaries—"This is my focus time."
- Communication boundaries—"This is the channel for urgent needs."
- Relational boundaries—"Here's what respect looks like for me."
- Personal boundaries—"I'm unavailable after this time."

Say it clearly. Hold it kindly. Lead it predictably.

Boundaries protect culture.

End-of-Week Reflection

Personal Leadership Check-In:

- Where did I set or protect a boundary this week?
- Where did I notice my boundaries slipping?
- How did people respond to my clarity?
- What do I need to keep practising to lead with boundaries that bring freedom?

WEEK 15:

RESPECT AND CONNECT ACROSS ORGANISATIONAL LEVELS

"Respect is one of the greatest expressions of love and leadership." —John C. Maxwell

Learn

Respect is not reserved for peers or those "above" us. True leadership respect flows to every person in the organisation.

Respect is not agreement—it's how we treat people regardless of their position, opinion, or performance.

In executive leadership, how you treat:

- The cleaner.
- The receptionist.
- The new graduate.
- The difficult stakeholder.

…says everything about your leadership.

Respect is the daily behaviour that builds relational capital across the organisation.

Respect is seen in:

- Your tone.
- Your time.
- Your attention.
- Your follow-through.

People may forget what you decided, but they will not forget how you made them feel.

Consider

Imagine an organisation where respect is positional—reserved for leaders or high performers only.

People disengage. Silos form. Trust fractures.

Now picture an organisation where respect is a cultural norm—where every voice matters, every role is valued, and every interaction reflects dignity.

Respect builds cultures of belonging and connection.

Let's Make It Real

Share a story of a leader you admired because they respected people regardless of role or status. What did that model teach you?

Alternatively, reflect on a time when a lack of respect damaged culture or trust. What was the ripple effect?

Invite reflection and sharing.

Discuss

Choose 2-3 of these for discussion.

- How would people at every level of this organisation describe our respect culture?
- Where are we modelling respect well—and where are we missing it?
- What behaviours build respect across organisational levels?
- What stories would our people tell about how we lead?
- How can we practise visible, tangible respect in our daily leadership rhythms?

Do

This week, practise Visible Respect.

Look for opportunities to:

- Slow down.
- Greet people by name.
- Ask a personal question.
- Say thank you.
- Follow through on a commitment.

Respect is built in the smallest interactions, but it lasts far beyond the moment.

End-of-Week Reflection

Personal Leadership Check-In:

- Where did I practise visible respect well this week?
- Where did I miss an opportunity to build connection?
- What feedback would people give me about how I show respect?
- What habits do I need to build into my leadership to lead a culture of respect every day?

WEEK 16:

GROWING AND TAKING RESPONSIBILITY USING THE EMPOWERMENT MODEL

"You cannot change your destination overnight, but you can change your direction overnight." —Jim Rohn

Learn

Growth-oriented leaders take responsibility for their own development.

They don't wait for circumstances to change—they change their approach.

The Empowerment Model provides a practical leadership tool for guiding both personal growth and coaching conversations with others.

Powerful leaders ask:

"What am I going to do about this?"

Not: *"Why is this happening to me?"*

Responsibility leads to growth. Avoidance leads to blame.

The Empowerment Model helps leaders think powerfully about themselves and coach others to do the same.

The Empowerment Model — 6 Leadership Steps

1. Empathy: "That sounds tough."
   (Acknowledge reality without rescuing.)

2. Empower: "What are you going to do?"
   (Hand responsibility back.)

3. Explore: "What have you tried already?"
   (Invite reflection and learning.)

4. Educate: "I have some ideas if you'd like them."
   (Offer input only if permission is given.)

5. Expect: "What will you do next?"
   (Create ownership of action.)

6. Encourage: "Let me know how it goes."
   (Support without controlling.)

Consider

Imagine an organisation where leaders fix problems for people instead of coaching them to think powerfully.

Dependency grows. Initiative dies. People wait to be rescued.

Now imagine a leadership culture where people are coached to reflect, own their part, and take action.

Empowerment builds capability and multiplies leaders.

Let's Make It Real

Share a story of a time when a leader coached you powerfully—not by fixing your problem, but by helping you take responsibility.

Alternatively, reflect on a time when rescuing leadership stifled growth or created frustration.

Invite the boardroom to reflect on where they see over-functioning or rescuing patterns showing up.

Discuss

Choose 2-3 of these for discussion.

- Where do we default to rescuing over empowering in this leadership team?
- What mindset or fear drives that behaviour?
- How would our culture change if we consistently used the Empowerment Model?
- Where do we need to get better at handing responsibility back to others?
- What would shift if our coaching conversations built ownership instead of dependence?

Do

This week, use the Empowerment Model in one coaching conversation.

When someone brings a problem to you:

1. Empathise: "That sounds tough."
2. Empower: "What are you going to do?"
3. Explore: "What have you tried already?"
4. Educate: "I have some ideas if you'd like them."
5. Expect: "What will you do next?"
6. Encourage: "Let me know how it goes."

Notice the shift in ownership and engagement.

Empowered people grow faster—and lead better.

End-of-Week Reflection

Personal Leadership Check-In:

- Where did I practise the Empowerment Model well this week?
- Where did I slip into rescuing or over-functioning?
- How did people respond when I handed responsibility back?
- What do I need to keep practising to lead a culture of powerful responsibility and growth?

WEEK 17:

LEARNING FROM MISTAKES WITH HUMILITY AND COURAGE

"Freedom is not worth having if it does not include the freedom to make mistakes." —Mahatma Gandhi

Learn

Healthy leadership cultures create space for mistakes—not because mistakes are the goal, but because mistakes are where the deepest growth happens.

Fear-based cultures hide mistakes.

Ownership cultures learn from them.

Mistakes handled well build trust, innovation, and resilience.

Mistakes handled poorly breed fear, blame, and disengagement.

Great leaders model:

- Humility: "I own what happened."
- Courage: "Here's what I've learned."
- Action: "Here's how I'll move forward."

Mistakes are not leadership failure—they are leadership formation.

Consider

Imagine a culture where mistakes are hidden because people fear blame or embarrassment.

- Learning stalls.
- Responsibility weakens.
- Trust erodes.

Now imagine a leadership culture where mistakes are owned quickly, shared openly, and used to drive learning.

- Teams problem-solve faster.
- Leaders model vulnerability.
- Trust deepens.

Growth requires freedom—and freedom requires permission to get it wrong sometimes.

Let's Make It Real

Share a story of a leadership mistake you made and what it taught you.

Alternatively, reflect on a time when a mistake in your organisation became a catalyst for growth and connection because of how it was handled.

Invite the team to reflect on where they see mistake-avoidance patterns showing up in their leadership.

Discuss

Choose 2-3 of these for discussion.

- What happens in this organisation when mistakes occur?
- How do we want people to experience mistakes and growth here?
- Where are we modelling humility and courage in our leadership responses?
- What stories do we need to tell more often about mistakes leading to growth?
- How do we create safe but responsible spaces for failure and learning?

Do

This week, practise modelling humility and courage around a mistake.

Whether small or large, say:

"Here's what I own in this."

"Here's what I've learned."

"Here's what I'll do next."

Invite others to reflect on their learning too.

Mistakes don't define culture—how we handle them does.

End-of-Week Reflection

Personal Leadership Check-In:

- Where did I model humility and courage around a mistake this week?
- Where did I notice fear or avoidance in myself or others?
- What learning came from this experience?
- What do I need to keep practising to lead a mistake-friendly, growth-driven culture?

WEEK 18:

COACHING FOR GROWTH—
DEVELOPING EMERGING LEADERS

*"Surround yourself with only people who are going
to lift you higher."* —Oprah Winfrey

Learn

Leadership is not just about what you build—it's about who you build.

Strong organisations don't just develop products or services—they develop people.

Great leaders are not defined by what they achieve alone--they are defined by who they raise up around them.

Coaching for growth means:

- Seeing potential in others.

- Creating space for learning.
- Asking better questions.
- Letting people lead.

Coaching is not telling people what to do—it's equipping them to figure it out.

It's slower in the short term, but exponential in the long term.

Consider

Imagine a leadership culture where development is reactive—only the people who shout the loudest or perform the most get investment.

Now imagine a leadership culture where growth is proactive—emerging leaders are noticed, supported, and stretched before they "prove" themselves.

Healthy leaders build a pipeline of healthy leaders.

Growth isn't left to chance—it's led with intention.

Let's Make It Real

Share a story of a leader who coached you into growth—not because they gave you all the answers, but because they believed in your capacity.

Alternatively, reflect on a time when someone gave you an opportunity before you felt ready. How did that shape you?

Invite the boardroom to reflect on who coached them, and who they need to coach next.

Discuss

Choose 2-3 of these for discussion.

- Who are the emerging leaders in our organisation we need to invest in?
- What's our current mindset about coaching—directive or developmental?
- Where do we need to slow down to coach more intentionally?
- How do we create structures that support coaching and feedback at every level?
- What opportunities are we holding that we need to hand to someone else?

Do

This week, take one step to coach an emerging leader.

Consider:

- Asking a growth-oriented question:
  "What are you learning right now?"
  "What's your next leadership challenge?"
- Handing them a stretch opportunity.
- Giving them feedback that builds clarity and confidence.
- Sharing a leadership resource or story from your journey.
- Committing to regular coaching check-ins.

Leadership growth is rarely accidental—it's almost always intentional.

End-of-Week Reflection

Personal Leadership Check-In:

- Who did I intentionally invest in or coach this week?
- How did I create space for their growth instead of filling it with my answers?
- Where did I see growth potential in someone I lead?
- What do I need to keep practising to develop a coaching culture in my leadership?

WEEK 19:

RESILIENCE AND STICKING WITH IT IN STRATEGIC LEADERSHIP

"Discipline is the bridge between goals and accomplishment."
—Jim Rohn

Learn

Leadership resilience is not about pushing through at all costs—it's about staying aligned with purpose when pressure comes.

Every leader faces seasons where momentum slows, resistance rises, or the work feels harder than expected.

Resilient leaders don't quit when it's hard—they dig deeper into:

- Purpose
- Disciplined habits
- Long-term vision

- Community support

In the boardroom, resilience shows up in:

- Sticking with cultural change when results are slow.
- Staying relationally present in conflict.
- Persisting with strategy when challenges arise.
- Staying true to values when shortcuts are tempting.

Resilience isn't doing everything––it's doing the right things consistently.

Consider

Imagine an organisation where leaders abandon initiatives, cultural values, or key projects the moment resistance comes.

People disengage. Trust erodes. Initiatives lose credibility.

Now imagine a culture where leaders are known for grit, consistency, and long-term focus—where sticking with purpose is celebrated more than reacting to pressure.

Resilience is not about speed—it's about faithfulness.

Let's Make It Real

Share a story of a time when sticking with something despite difficulty produced long-term fruit in your leadership or organisation.

Alternatively, reflect on a time when a lack of resilience or follow-through damaged culture or trust.

Invite reflection on where the team is being called to lead with greater resilience right now.

Discuss

Choose 2-3 of these for discussion.

- Where are we currently leading through resistance or challenge?
- What behaviours signal resilience to our teams?
- Where do we need to stay the course more consistently?
- What disciplines or rhythms support our resilience as leaders?
- How do we celebrate perseverance and process, not just fast results?

Do

This week, identify one area where you need to practise resilient leadership.

- Revisit the "why" behind your strategy or decision.
- Reinforce your commitment publicly:
  "We're staying the course because this matters."
- Celebrate small wins along the way.
- Strengthen your leadership rhythms—rest, reflection, team connection—so you lead from overflow, not burnout.

Resilience is not loud—it's steady.

End-of-Week Reflection

Personal Leadership Check-In:

- Where did I practise resilient leadership this week?
- Where did I feel pressure to quit, react, or give up?
- What sustained me in those moments?
- What do I need to keep practising to lead a culture of long-term, resilient leadership?

WEEK 20:

JOYFUL RESPONSIBILITY—THE CULTURE OF OWNERSHIP

"With great freedom comes great responsibility."
—Eleanor Roosevelt

Learn

Responsibility in leadership is not a burden—it's a privilege.

Joyful responsibility means carrying your role, your influence, and your actions with pride, not pressure.

Ownership is the foundation of trust and culture.

When leaders carry responsibility with joy:

- Teams follow their example.
- Accountability becomes inspiring, not punishing.

- People take pride in their work.
- Initiative grows naturally.

A culture of ownership says: *"I get to do this, not I have to do this."*

Responsibility doesn't take away freedom—it creates it.

Consider

Imagine a leadership culture where responsibility feels heavy, resentful, or begrudging.

People avoid ownership. Tasks get passed around. Problems linger.

Now imagine a leadership culture where responsibility is carried with joy, commitment, and self-leadership.

People say: *"This matters and I want to give my best to it."*

Joyful responsibility doesn't mean everything is easy—it means you lead with purpose and pride.

Let's Make It Real

Share a story of a time when taking ownership brought you energy, fulfilment, or pride, even in a hard season.

Alternatively, reflect on a time when ownership was absent and the burden of leadership fell unevenly across a team.

Invite reflection on where the organisation needs to increase ownership right now.

Discuss

Choose 2-3 of these for discussion.

- How is responsibility currently experienced in this leadership team—joyful or heavy?
- Where have we unintentionally created a culture of blame or avoidance?
- How do we lead with joy and ownership, even when work is hard?
- Where do we need to raise the bar of personal responsibility across the organisation?
- What language, rhythms, or behaviours reinforce ownership in our culture?

Do

This week, practise Joyful Responsibility.

- Model ownership language:
  "I own this."
  "This is my part to carry."
  "Let me clean up my side of the street."
- Celebrate visible ownership in others.
- Hand back responsibility where you've been over-functioning.
- Lead from overflow—prioritise rhythms that sustain you so that responsibility feels joyful, not draining.

Joyful responsibility is a leadership multiplier.

End-of-Week Reflection

Personal Leadership Check-In:

- Where did I practise joyful responsibility this week?

- Where did I feel resentment, avoidance, or frustration—and what triggered that?

- How did my language or behaviour model ownership to my team?

- What do I need to keep practising to lead a culture of joyful, powerful responsibility?

PART THREE

DEMONSTRATING GENUINE RESTORATION

Every leader makes mistakes—great leaders make things right.

This section equips leaders to repair, restore, and rebuild trust when things go wrong. Genuine restoration is about creating cultures where feedback, apology, forgiveness, and second chances are not rare but normal.

Trust is never built in perfection—it's built in the repair process. This section helps leaders navigate difficult moments with courage, humility, and connection, strengthening culture for the long term.

WEEK 21:

THE ART OF APOLOGY IN EXECUTIVE LEADERSHIP

"It's important to be able to say sorry, even if you find it really hard." —Chilli (Bluey's Mom)

Learn

The most trusted leaders are not the ones who never get it wrong—they're the ones who know how to make it right.

Apology is a powerful leadership tool, not a sign of weakness.

Apologising well does not diminish your authority—it strengthens it.

Poor apologies avoid responsibility or minimise the impact:

- "Sorry if you felt that way..."
- "I'm sorry, but..."

Powerful apologies own the action and the impact:

- "I got that wrong."
- "I see how my actions affected you."
- "Here's what I'm doing to repair this."

Great leaders clean up their mess with courage and clarity.

Consider

Imagine a leadership culture where mistakes are ignored or defended, and where apologies are rare.

Trust erodes. Resentment grows. Culture suffers.

Now imagine a leadership culture where owning mistakes and repairing connection is normal.

People know their leaders are human and real.

This creates loyalty, safety, and integrity.

Let's Make It Real

Share a story of a time when someone apologised to you well. What did it unlock for you?

Alternatively, reflect on a time when a poor apology (or no apology) damaged trust or connection.

Invite the boardroom to reflect on their experiences of powerful apologies in leadership.

Discuss

Choose 2-3 of these for discussion.

- How is apology modelled and practised in this leadership team?
- Where do we need to get better at owning and repairing mistakes?
- What impact would normalising healthy apology have on our organisational culture?
- Where might an apology be needed right now—to a team, a colleague, or a stakeholder?

Do

This week, practise the Art of Apology where appropriate.

Use the 3 Elements of a Powerful Apology:

1. Own It: "I got this wrong..."
2. Acknowledge Impact: "I can see how this affected you..."
3. Action to Repair: "Here's what I will do to make this right..."

Clean up your side of the street.

Watch what it does to your culture.

End-of-Week Reflection

Personal Leadership Check-In:

- Where did I practise a powerful apology this week?

- Where did I avoid or minimise ownership, and what was the impact?
- How did people respond to my apology?
- What do I need to keep practising to lead a culture of courage, humility, and repair?

WEEK 22:

FORGIVENESS AND MOVING FORWARD ORGANISATIONALLY

"Forgiveness is not an occasional act; it is a permanent attitude." —Martin Luther King Jr.

Learn

Forgiveness in leadership is not forgetting—it's releasing.

Forgiveness doesn't excuse poor behaviour or remove accountability.

Forgiveness removes bitterness so growth can happen.

In executive leadership, unforgiveness shows up as:

- Resentment between teams.
- Holding past mistakes over people.
- Withholding trust or opportunity.

- Avoiding relationship repair.

Forgiveness is essential to healthy leadership because it releases both the leader and the organisation from being stuck in the past.

Forgiveness says:

"I see the impact, I acknowledge the reality, and I choose to release the offence so we can move forward."

Consider

Imagine a leadership culture where mistakes are remembered more than growth.

Where people are defined by their worst day, not their best potential.

Now imagine a leadership culture where accountability is real, but forgiveness is normal.

Where mistakes are addressed but not weaponised.

Forgiveness creates freedom—for individuals and for teams.

Let's Make It Real

Share a story of a time when you forgave a leader or a colleague. What did it unlock for you?

Alternatively, reflect on a time when you were forgiven and how that act of grace impacted your growth.

Invite the boardroom to reflect on where unforgiveness or bitterness may be limiting growth or connection.

Discuss

Choose 2-3 of these for discussion.

- How is forgiveness practised in our leadership culture?
- Where might we be holding onto resentment or past mistakes as individuals or teams?
- What happens to culture when unforgiveness is normalised?
- What would it look like to model forgiveness in leadership while maintaining accountability?
- Who do I need to forgive (or seek forgiveness from) to lead more freely?

Do

This week, practise forgiveness where it's needed.

Reflect honestly:

- Where am I holding onto offence?
- What is this costing me or the team?
- What conversations might I need to have, even if just to release this internally?

Say:

"I release this. I'm not carrying this into our future leadership together."

Forgiveness creates space for growth.

End-of-Week Reflection

Personal Leadership Check-In:

- Where did I practise forgiveness this week?

- Where did I notice resentment or bitterness holding me back?

- How did forgiveness create freedom for me or for others?

- What do I need to keep practising to lead with grace, accountability, and freedom?

WEEK 23:

RESTORING TRUST AFTER LEADERSHIP MISSTEPS

"Trust is choosing to make something important to you vulnerable to the actions of someone else." —Brené Brown

Learn

Every leader makes mistakes.

The question is not: *"Will I break trust?"*

The question is: *"Will I repair trust?"*

Trust is built slowly, but it can be restored intentionally.

Restoring trust requires:

- Ownership of what happened.
- Empathy for the impact.

- Predictability in future behaviour.
- Patience—because trust rebuilds over time.

Trust is not rebuilt through words alone—it's rebuilt through predictable, trustworthy behaviour.

In leadership, the faster you own it, the faster you can rebuild.

Consider

Imagine a leadership culture where broken trust is ignored or covered over.

People remember.

Culture suffers.

Disconnection grows.

Now imagine a culture where trust repair is normalised.

Leaders say:

"I got this wrong."

"Here's how I'm making it right."

"Let's walk this out together."

That's how relational capital is restored and trust is rebuilt.

Let's Make It Real

Share a story of a time when a leader restored trust with you. What behaviours helped rebuild connection?

Alternatively, reflect on a time when trust wasn't repaired. What did that cost a team or organisation?

Invite the boardroom to reflect on how trust has been handled in their leadership journey.

Discuss

Choose 2-3 of these for discussion.

- What's our process for restoring trust when it's been broken?
- How well do we model trust repair as an executive team?
- Where might there be unrepaired trust gaps in our organisation right now?
- What behaviours are essential for restoring trust here?
- What story do we want our people to tell about how we handle mistakes and trust?

Do

This week, practise intentional trust repair where needed.

Use the Trust Repair Model:

1. Own It: "This is what I got wrong."
2. Empathise: "I can see how this impacted you."
3. Repair: "Here's what I'm doing to restore this."
4. Stay Consistent: Trust builds again over time.

Leadership credibility is not in perfection—it's in your capacity to repair well.

End-of-Week Reflection

Personal Leadership Check-In:

- Where did I practise trust repair this week?

- Where might I still need to own something or restore connection?

- How did people respond to my ownership and consistency?

- What do I need to keep practising to lead a culture where trust is built and rebuilt with integrity?

WEEK 24:

SECOND CHANCES IN PERFORMANCE AND LEADERSHIP DEVELOPMENT

"Don't think there are no second chances. Life always offers you a second chance… It's called tomorrow."
—Nicholas Sparks

Learn

Great leaders don't just give feedback—they give second chances.

Second chances are not about lowering standards—they are about raising people.

In healthy leadership cultures:

- Failure is never final.
- Feedback is followed by opportunity.

- Mistakes are met with responsibility and another shot at growth.

Second chances communicate:

- "I see your potential beyond your performance."
- "I believe in your ability to learn, grow, and lead."
- "I will hold you accountable—but I will also stay in your corner."

This builds loyalty, growth, and resilience.

Consider

Imagine a leadership culture where mistakes equal disqualification.

People stop taking risks. Innovation dies. Teams hide failures.

Now imagine a leadership culture where accountability is strong, but grace is stronger.

People take ownership. Learn quickly. Step up with new courage.

Second chances teach people how to lead powerfully, not perfectly.

Let's Make It Real

Share a story of a time when you were given a second chance in your leadership journey. What did it unlock for you?

Alternatively, reflect on a time when giving a second chance to someone else produced unexpected growth or loyalty.

Invite the boardroom to reflect on their posture toward failure, grace, and growth.

Discuss

Choose 2-3 of these for discussion.

- How does our leadership team practise giving second chances?
- What boundaries are important in offering second chances well?
- Where have second chances produced growth and trust in our organisation?
- Where might fear of failure be limiting people's ownership or development?
- How do we lead a culture that values both accountability and grace?

Do

This week, look for a person or situation that needs a well-framed second chance.

- Offer clear feedback.
- Set clear expectations.
- Communicate belief in their potential.
- Support them in their next step.

Say:

"I believe in your ability to own this and do it better moving forward."

Second chances build future leaders.

End-of-Week Reflection

Personal Leadership Check-In:

- Where did I offer a second chance this week, and how did I frame it?

- Where did I notice a fear of failure limiting ownership in myself or others?

- How did my posture of grace and accountability affect culture this week?

- What do I need to keep practising to lead a culture of growth, responsibility, and second chances?

WEEK 25:

TAKING RESPONSIBILITY FOR ORGANISATIONAL CULTURE

"If you own this story, you get to write the ending."
—Brené Brown

Learn

Culture is not a mission statement. Culture is what happens every day in your organisation.

Leaders are always creating culture intentionally or unintentionally. Every conversation, every decision, every behaviour reinforces your culture.

Healthy culture doesn't happen because of great vision statements—it happens because of great ownership.

Leaders who take responsibility for culture say:

- "Culture is my job, not someone else's problem."
- "What I tolerate becomes normal."
- "What I model becomes multiplied."

If you want to change culture, start with yourself.

Consider

Imagine a leadership team where culture is outsourced—left to HR, new programs, or slogans on the wall.

Now imagine a leadership team where every leader owns the environment they create.

Disrespect is addressed. Positivity is modelled. Feedback is normalised. Trust is built. Responsibility is carried with joy.

That's the culture people remember and stay for.

Let's Make It Real

Share a story of a time when someone shaped culture in a powerful way through their behaviour, not their title.

Alternatively, reflect on a moment when poor leadership culture was tolerated and what it cost the team.

Invite the boardroom to reflect on where they see culture drift happening and where ownership needs to increase.

Discuss

Choose 2-3 of these for discussion.

- Where is culture healthy and vibrant in our organisation right now?
- Where is culture drifting and why?
- What behaviours are being tolerated that do not reflect who we want to be?
- What do I need to own in shaping the culture I'm part of?
- How do we hold each other accountable for creating the culture we want to see?

Do

This week, take ownership of one culture-building behaviour.

Choose to:

- Address a behaviour that doesn't align with your values.
- Celebrate a behaviour that reinforces your culture.
- Name the kind of culture you're committed to creating—out loud and often.
- Lead yourself well, because your behaviour is the most powerful culture-shaping tool you have.

End-of-Week Reflection

Personal Leadership Check-In:

- Where did I take ownership of culture this week?

- Where did I tolerate something I should have addressed?
- How did my actions shape the culture of my team or organisation?
- What do I need to keep practising to lead a culture of responsibility, clarity, and health?

WEEK 26:

POWERFUL LEADERSHIP FRIENDSHIPS & ALLIES

"Your reputation is what people say about you when you're not in the room." —Jeff Bezos

Learn

Leadership can feel lonely, but it should never be isolated.

Healthy leaders cultivate powerful friendships and allies who:

- Speak truth with kindness.
- Celebrate wins without competition.
- Hold them accountable without judgement.
- Stand with them in challenge and success.

Powerful friendships in leadership aren't about comfort—they're about sharpening.

Leadership friendships thrive when built on:

- Trust
- Vulnerability
- Accountability
- Respect
- Shared values

Leadership is a team sport, not a solo performance.

Consider

Imagine a leadership culture where isolation is normal—where leaders compete, compare, and protect their image at the expense of connection.

Now imagine a culture where leaders build strong internal and external alliances—where peers encourage, challenge, and support one another to lead well.

Powerful friendships multiply resilience, growth, and emotional health.

They create safe places for honest reflection before burnout or poor decisions happen.

Let's Make It Real

Share a story of a leadership friendship or ally that has shaped your growth. How did they impact your leadership journey?

Alternatively, reflect on a time when leadership isolation became costly for yourself or someone else.

Invite the boardroom to reflect on who they need in their corner for the next season of leadership.

Discuss

Choose 2-3 of these for discussion.

- How do we model healthy leadership friendships and alliances in this organisation?
- Where are we leading in isolation and what is that costing us?
- Who do I need to intentionally connect with or reach out to in this season?
- What makes a leadership friendship powerful, not just comfortable?
- How can we cultivate a leadership culture of encouragement, accountability, and trust?

Do

This week, invest in one powerful leadership connection.

Choose to:

- Reach out to a mentor, coach, or peer leader.
- Send encouragement or gratitude to someone who has shaped you.
- Create space for honest conversation with a trusted colleague.
- Name what you need in a leadership ally or friend for this next season.

Powerful leadership doesn't happen alone.

End-of-Week Reflection

Personal Leadership Check-In:

- Where did I invest in a leadership friendship or ally this week?

- Where did I notice isolation, and what needs to shift?

- How did connection and encouragement affect my leadership energy?

- What do I need to keep practising to lead with relational strength, humility, and courage?

WEEK 27:

BECOMING A POWERFUL PERSON IN EVERY ROOM

"Powerful people take responsibility for their lives and choices. Powerful people choose who they want to be with, what they are going to pursue in life, and how they are going to go after it."
—Danny Silk

Learn

True power in leadership is not about titles or position—it's about self-leadership.

A powerful person is someone who takes full responsibility for:

- Their words
- Their choices
- Their emotions

- Their behaviour
- Their influence

Powerful people lead themselves well regardless of:

- Who else is in the room
- How others are behaving
- What pressures arise
- What emotions surface

Powerless leaders blame circumstances, control others, or avoid responsibility.

Powerful leaders say: *"No one else is responsible for me. I lead myself."*

This is the foundation of sustainable, authentic leadership.

Consider

Imagine a leadership culture where people lead reactively, controlled by others' behaviour or circumstances.

Now imagine a leadership culture where people lead themselves first, modelling self-regulation, integrity, boundaries, and respect.

Powerful people create powerful cultures.

When leaders are responsible for their own emotions and behaviour, trust and freedom flourish.

Let's Make It Real

Share a story of a time when you witnessed powerful leadership in action—not because of control, but because of self-leadership.

Alternatively, reflect on a moment when you personally shifted from reacting to owning your actions as a leader. What changed?

Invite reflection on where the team needs to practise powerful leadership right now.

Discuss

Choose 2-3 of these for discussion.

- How would people describe our leadership team—powerful or reactive?
- Where do I personally need to grow in self-leadership right now?
- What does it look like to be a powerful person in hard conversations or high-pressure environments?
- How do we create a culture where powerful self-leadership is normal?
- What habits support me in becoming a powerful leader in every room?

Do

This week, practise powerful self-leadership in one key situation.

Choose to:

- Respond, not react.
- Own your emotions.
- Set healthy boundaries.
- Take responsibility for your words and actions.

- Model calm, clarity, and consistency regardless of the room dynamics.

Say to yourself: *"I am responsible for me. No one else is."*

Powerful leaders lead themselves—then lead others.

End-of-Week Reflection

Personal Leadership Check-In:

- Where did I practise powerful self-leadership this week?
- Where did I notice reactive or powerless patterns, and what triggered them?
- How did my behaviour shape the environment I was in?
- What do I need to keep practising to become a powerful person in every room I lead?

WEEK 28:

RESTORING SELF-RESPECT IN SEASONS OF LEADERSHIP FATIGUE

"I cannot conceive of a greater loss than the loss of one's self-respect." —Mahatma Gandhi

Learn

Self-respect is the foundation of sustainable leadership.

When leaders lose self-respect, they:

- Compromise their values.
- Lead from exhaustion, not conviction.
- Tolerate poor behaviour (from themselves or others).
- Disconnect from their purpose.
- Erode trust—starting with themselves.

Restoring self-respect isn't about perfection—it's about realignment.

It's saying:

"This is who I am."

"This is what I value."

"This is how I will lead, starting with myself."

Healthy leaders lead themselves with the same respect they offer to others.

Self-respect fuels:

- Boundaries.
- Healthy habits.
- Wise decision-making.
- Leadership longevity.

Consider

Imagine a leadership culture where people sacrifice their well-being, boundaries, or integrity to keep up appearances or meet expectations.

Over time, this erodes health, trust, and influence.

Now imagine a leadership culture where people model self-respect by:

- Leading sustainably.
- Resting strategically.
- Owning mistakes without shame.

- Aligning their behaviour with their values, even under pressure.

Restored self-respect strengthens teams—because leaders are strong within themselves.

Let's Make It Real

Share a story of a time when you lost connection with your own self-respect, and how you restored it.

Alternatively, reflect on a leader you admire who led from self-respect and courage, even in hard seasons.

Invite the boardroom to reflect on how leadership fatigue may be impacting their personal alignment right now.

Discuss

Choose 2-3 of these for discussion.

- Where am I currently out of alignment with my values or self-respect?
- What habits or patterns are eroding my leadership health?
- How would my team describe my example of self-respect and sustainability?
- What do I need to change or commit to in order to restore self-respect?
- How can we as a team support healthy leadership rhythms and integrity for one another?

Do

This week, take one action to restore or protect your self-respect.

Consider:

- Revisiting your personal values.
- Resetting a boundary that's been compromised.
- Owning a behaviour that's out of alignment.
- Creating space for rest or reflection.
- Saying no to something so you can say yes to what matters most.

Healthy leadership flows from self-respect.

End-of-Week Reflection

Personal Leadership Check-In:

- Where did I practise or restore self-respect this week?
- Where did I notice fatigue or disconnection, and what caused it?
- How did realigning with my values impact my leadership?
- What do I need to keep practising to lead with integrity, health, and self-respect?

WEEK 29:

TAKING INITIATIVE WITH THE EMPOWERMENT MODEL

"Action cures fear." —Mel Robbins

Learn

Initiative is a hallmark of powerful leadership.

Powerful leaders don't wait for permission to take action—they take responsibility for their next step.

The Empowerment Model helps leaders coach initiative in others without rescuing or micromanaging.

It creates a culture where people own their problems, generate solutions, and act with confidence.

The Empowerment Model has 6 clear steps to guide yourself or others through challenge:

The Empowerment Model:

1. Empathy: "That sounds tough."
   (Acknowledge reality without taking ownership of the problem.)

2. Empower: "What are you going to do?"
   (Hand responsibility back—invite ownership.)

3. Explore: "What have you tried so far?"
   (Encourage reflection and learning.)

4. Educate: "I have some ideas if you'd like them."
   (Offer wisdom only with permission.)

5. Expect: "What will you do next?"
   (Create accountability for their next step.)

6. Encourage: "Let me know how it goes."
   (Stay supportive without taking over.)

Consider

Imagine a leadership culture where people bring problems but never solutions.

Where decision-making is escalated unnecessarily.

Now imagine a culture where initiative is normal—where leaders and teams use the Empowerment Model daily.

Problems are owned. Responsibility is shared. Action is taken quickly and wisely.

Empowerment is not fixing things for people—it's equipping them to lead themselves.

Let's Make It Real

Share a story of a time when someone empowered you instead of rescuing you. What did that unlock for your growth and leadership?

Alternatively, reflect on where over-functioning or micromanaging has stunted initiative in your team or organisation.

Invite reflection on where empowerment is most needed in your current leadership context.

Discuss

Choose 2-3 of these for discussion.

- Where do we tend to rescue or fix instead of empowering others?
- What behaviour patterns are limiting initiative in our culture?
- How would using the Empowerment Model consistently shift our leadership culture?
- Where do I need to take initiative right now, rather than waiting for permission or perfect conditions?
- How do we build a culture where ownership and action are normal?

Do

This week, practise the Empowerment Model in one coaching conversation, either in a 1:1 or in a team environment:

1. Empathise: "That sounds tough."
2. Empower: "What are you going to do?"

3. Explore: "What have you tried already?"

4. Educate: "I have some ideas if you'd like them."

5. Expect: "What will you do next?"

6. Encourage: "Let me know how it goes."

Coach people to think, act, and lead powerfully.

Model initiative yourself—act where action is needed.

End-of-Week Reflection

Personal Leadership Check-In:

- Where did I practise using the Empowerment Model this week?

- Where did I notice myself rescuing or over-functioning, and what caused that?

- How did people respond when I empowered them to lead themselves?

- What do I need to keep practising to build a leadership culture of initiative, ownership, and action?

WEEK 30:

BEING A CULTURE-SETTING ROLE MODEL

"If you want to bring happiness to the whole world, go home and love your family." —Mother Teresa

Learn

Every leader is a culture-setter.

Whether you intend to or not, how you show up, how you speak, how you behave sets the tone for your organisation.

Being a role model isn't about being perfect—it's about being consistent.

Great leaders know:

- The smallest behaviours create the biggest impact.

- People are watching and learning from their example.
- Influence flows not just from what you say, but from what you do every day.

Culture is not created in vision statements—it's created in ordinary moments.

Role modelling the culture you want to see means:

- Leading yourself first.
- Practising respect always.
- Holding boundaries clearly.
- Owning mistakes openly.
- Treating people with dignity regardless of position.

Consider

Imagine a leadership culture where leaders expect behaviours from others they do not practise themselves.

Hypocrisy damages trust faster than any policy can repair it.

Now imagine a leadership culture where the top leaders go first.

They lead themselves with integrity. They communicate with kindness. They practise accountability. They set clear expectations and meet them personally.

People don't leave organisations—they leave cultures.

Cultures rise and fall on the everyday example of their leaders.

Let's Make It Real

Share a story of a leader you admired because of their example. What did they model that shaped your leadership?

Alternatively, reflect on a time when leadership behaviour failed to align with organisational values. What impact did that have?

Invite reflection on where the team needs to lift their leadership example.

Discuss

Choose 2-3 of these for discussion.

- What do I want my leadership to be known for even when I'm not in the room?

- Where am I modelling the culture we want to see, and where am I missing it?

- What small behaviours are most powerful in shaping our leadership culture?

- How would our people describe the example set by our leadership team?

- What do I need to start, stop, or strengthen to lead with integrity and consistency?

Do

This week, choose one area where you will intentionally lift your example.

Consider:

- Practising deeper listening.
- Setting clearer boundaries.
- Owning a mistake publicly.
- Celebrating others visibly.
- Leading with calm and clarity under pressure.

Say:

"Culture starts with me."

Leadership is stewardship of trust, influence, and culture.

End-of-Week Reflection

Personal Leadership Check-In:

- Where did I practise culture-setting leadership this week?
- Where did I notice a gap between what I value and what I practised?
- How did my behaviour shape trust, safety, or clarity in my team?
- What do I need to keep practising to lead as a culture-setting role model?

PART FOUR

LEGACY LEADERSHIP

Leadership is never about one person—it's about raising others.

This final section focuses on building a culture where leadership is multiplied, not hoarded. Great leaders invest in others, hand over opportunities, and develop the next generation of leaders with wisdom and generosity.

This section equips executives to build systems, habits, and mindsets that empower people at every level—creating cultures that outlast personalities and thrive beyond seasons of change.

WEEK 31:

LEADING THROUGH SERVICE— SERVING BEYOND SELF

"Only a life lived for others is a life worthwhile."
—Albert Einstein

Learn

True leadership is never about self-promotion—it's about service.

Serving leadership isn't weak. It's the strongest, most influential posture a leader can take.

Serving leaders ask:

- "How can I help others succeed?"
- "How can I remove barriers for my team?"
- "How can I elevate others' voices?"
- "How can I use my influence for their good?"

Serving leadership looks like:

- Listening before speaking.
- Acting before demanding.
- Owning mistakes before blaming.
- Encouraging before correcting.
- Giving credit before taking it.

This kind of leadership multiplies trust, loyalty, and ownership at every level.

Consider

Imagine a leadership culture where people fight for position, recognition, or personal advancement.

Teams become competitive rather than collaborative. Trust erodes. Energy is spent protecting self-image rather than building others.

Now imagine a leadership culture where the most influential leaders are the most servant-hearted.

They model humility. They lead with strength and grace. They champion others—even when no one sees it.

This kind of culture attracts, develops, and retains powerful people.

Let's Make It Real

Share a story of a leader you've admired for their service-oriented leadership. How did their behaviour shape the team or organisation?

Alternatively, reflect on a time when serving others—not seeking position—created unexpected influence in your leadership journey.

Invite the boardroom to reflect on where service-based leadership is needed most right now.

Discuss

Choose 2-3 of these for discussion.

- Where do we currently lead well through service, and where do we drift toward self-preservation?
- What practical behaviours demonstrate serving leadership in this organisation?
- Where have we seen leadership influence grow because of service and humility?
- How do we multiply this culture of service in our teams?
- Who needs me to serve them more intentionally this week, not just lead them?

Do

This week, practise Leading Through Service.

Choose one intentional act of service within your sphere of leadership:

- Remove a barrier for someone.
- Do a task that would normally fall outside your role without fanfare.
- Celebrate someone else's win publicly.

- Create space for someone else's voice in a meeting.
- Ask: *"What do you need most from me right now?"*

Serving leaders multiply influence without needing control.

End-of-Week Reflection

Personal Leadership Check-In:

- Where did I lead through service this week?
- Where did I notice the temptation to lead for self over service, and what triggered that?
- How did serving others change the tone or connection within my team?
- What do I need to keep practising to lead with strength, humility, and a heart for others?

WEEK 32:

MENTORING AND DEVELOPING FUTURE LEADERS

"Leadership is not about being in charge. It is about taking care of those in your charge." —Simon Sinek

Learn

One of the highest callings of leadership is to raise up other leaders.

Your leadership legacy isn't just what you build—it's who you build.

Mentoring is about:

- Investing time and energy into others' growth.
- Sharing wisdom gained through experience.
- Creating space for emerging leaders to learn, lead, and make mistakes.
- Believing in people before they believe in themselves.

Future-focused leaders ask:

- "Who am I raising up?"
- "Who is watching me lead?"
- "Who am I handing opportunity to?"
- "Who will carry this culture when I'm gone?"

Mentoring doesn't slow down progress—it multiplies it.

Consider

Imagine a leadership culture where future leaders emerge only by accident—where no one is intentionally investing in the next generation.

Critical knowledge is lost. Cultural momentum fades. Teams become reactive instead of strategic.

Now imagine a leadership culture where every leader is a mentor.

Wisdom flows freely. Mistakes become learning moments. Emerging leaders step into growth with confidence.

Future-ready organisations don't wait for leaders to appear—they develop them on purpose.

Let's Make It Real

Share a story of a leader who mentored you. What did their investment unlock for your leadership journey?

Alternatively, reflect on a time when mentoring someone else created unexpected growth for them and for you.

Invite the boardroom to reflect on who they are intentionally developing right now.

Discuss

Choose 2-3 of these for discussion.

- Who am I currently mentoring formally or informally?
- Where do I need to make time or space for intentional leadership development?
- What opportunities am I holding onto that I could hand to someone else?
- How do we build a mentoring culture across all levels of this organisation?
- What behaviours model mentoring well in our leadership team?

Do

This week, take a practical step toward mentoring or developing a future leader.

Consider:

- Scheduling a mentoring conversation or check-in.
- Sharing a leadership lesson or resource from your journey.
- Handing someone else a stretch opportunity.
- Asking a growth-oriented question: *"What's the next step in your leadership development?"*

Great leaders build others, not just outcomes.

End-of-Week Reflection

Personal Leadership Check-In:

- Where did I invest in mentoring or developing a leader this week?
- Where did I notice resistance to handing over opportunity, and what triggered that?
- How did my investment shape connection or growth?
- What do I need to keep practising to lead a culture of development, generosity, and future leadership?

WEEK 33:

PRIORITY MANAGEMENT FOR EXECUTIVE EFFECTIVENESS

"The key is not to prioritise what's on your schedule, but to schedule your priorities." —Stephen Covey

Learn

Leaders don't manage time—they manage priorities.

Every leader has the same 24 hours. What sets great leaders apart is clarity on what matters most.

Priority management is about:

- Saying yes to the right things.
- Saying no with integrity.
- Protecting space for deep, strategic work.
- Guarding what fuels you, not just what drains you.

Busyness is not a badge of honour—clarity is.

Executives who manage priorities well model focus, discipline, and intentional leadership.

Leaders who don't manage priorities drift into:

- Reactivity over strategy.
- Firefighting over long-term building.
- Burnout over sustainability.

Consider

Imagine a leadership culture where busyness is praised, but effectiveness is low.

People react to urgency rather than leading with clarity. Work expands to fill the day. Strategic growth is delayed.

Now imagine a leadership culture where priorities are visible, protected, and shared.

Meetings have purpose. Workflows are focused. Leaders know and protect their highest value tasks.

This creates clarity, momentum, and sustainable performance.

Let's Make It Real

Share a story of a time when clear priority management created significant results in your leadership or organisation.

Alternatively, reflect on a season of leadership where poor priority management led to frustration or fatigue, and what shifted.

Invite the boardroom to reflect on how priorities are managed personally and organisationally.

Discuss

Choose 2-3 of these for discussion.

- What currently defines our priorities—urgency or clarity?
- Where are we most effective at protecting what matters most?
- Where do we need to realign our focus as a leadership team?
- What does healthy priority management look like in our leadership rhythms?
- How do we help our teams focus on the right things, not just more things?

Do

This week, practise Priority Management.

Consider:

- Rewriting your task list. What's most valuable, not just most urgent?
- Blocking time for strategic thinking, planning, or creative work.
- Saying no to something that doesn't align with your highest priorities.
- Asking your team: *"What's the most important thing I can do for this organisation right now?"*

Priority management is leadership stewardship.

End-of-Week Reflection

Personal Leadership Check-In:

- Where did I practise effective priority management this week?

- Where did I notice drift into reactivity or busyness, and why?

- How did clarity of focus affect my leadership energy and effectiveness?

- What do I need to keep practising to lead with clarity, focus, and sustainability?

WEEK 34:

STRATEGIC PROBLEM-SOLVING AS A LEADERSHIP TEAM

"We cannot solve our problems with the same thinking we used when we created them." —Albert Einstein

Learn

Strategic problem-solving is not about quick fixes—it's about collaborative thinking, creativity, and ownership.

In executive leadership, problems are rarely isolated. They are complex, multi-layered, and require diverse perspectives.

Great leadership teams solve problems by:

- Slowing down before reacting.
- Clarifying the real problem, not just the symptoms.
- Asking powerful questions.

- Involving the right people at the right time.
- Owning both the problem and the solution.

Strategic problem-solving builds trust, capability, and healthy ownership across the organisation.

Consider

Imagine a leadership culture where problem-solving is reactive and top-down.

Leaders move fast but miss root causes. Solutions create more problems. People feel disempowered.

Now imagine a leadership culture where problem-solving is collaborative and strategic.

Leaders ask: *"What's really going on here?"* Teams own the process together. Solutions are creative, sustainable, and shared.

Healthy leadership teams lead with wisdom, not just speed.

Let's Make It Real

Share a story of a time when strategic, collaborative problem-solving produced breakthrough results. What behaviours made it possible?

Alternatively, reflect on a time when poor problem-solving created frustration or more complexity, and what you learned.

Invite the boardroom to reflect on how they currently approach complex challenges.

Discuss

Choose 2-3 of these for discussion.

- How do we approach problem-solving in this leadership team—reactive or strategic?

- Where are we solving symptoms rather than root causes?

- Who needs to be included more often in our problem-solving conversations?

- What behaviours build trust and ownership during problem-solving?

- How do we create a culture where people bring problems with solutions, not just complaints?

Do

This week, practise Strategic Problem-Solving as a team.

Choose a current challenge and apply this framework:

1. Clarify the Problem: *What's really going on here?"*

2. Identify Impact: *"Who is affected and how?"*

3. Explore Solutions: *"What have we tried or considered already?"*

4. Assign Ownership: *"Who will lead next steps?"*

5. Communicate Clearly: *"Who else needs to know?"*

6. Reflect and Learn: *"What did we learn from this process?"*

Strategic leadership solves problems in a way that builds people and doesn't just fix issues.

End-of-Week Reflection

Personal Leadership Check-In:

- Where did I practise strategic problem-solving this week?
- Where did I notice reactivity or short-term thinking in myself or others?
- How did collaborative problem-solving build trust or ownership in my team?
- What do I need to keep practising to lead a culture of wise, collaborative problem-solving?

WEEK 35:

EMPOWERING OTHERS TO OWN THEIR CHOICES

"The price of greatness is responsibility."
—Winston Churchill

Learn

Empowering leadership is not about making choices for people—it's about equipping them to own their choices.

Ownership is the foundation of high-performing teams.

Leaders who constantly rescue or decide for others create dependency.

Leaders who empower others to think, choose, and act create capability.

Empowering leadership sounds like.

- "What do you want to do about this?"
- "What choice will move you forward?"
- "What outcome do you want to own?"

Empowerment is both a mindset and a skill—it multiplies confidence, initiative, and accountability.

Consider

Imagine a leadership culture where decisions are bottlenecked at the top.

People avoid risk. Teams wait for instructions. Growth stalls.

Now imagine a leadership culture where people are trusted to own their choices and their impact.

Leaders guide but don't control. Teams bring solutions, not just problems. Ownership flows down through the organisation.

Empowering leadership builds capacity and creates leaders at every level.

Let's Make It Real

Share a story of a time when someone empowered you to own a choice even when it stretched you. How did that experience shape your growth?

Alternatively, reflect on a time when you empowered someone else, and what it unlocked in their leadership journey.

Invite the boardroom to reflect on where empowerment is most needed in their leadership right now.

Discuss

Choose 2-3 of these for discussion.

- Where do we need to practise empowering leadership more consistently?

- What behaviours in our culture reinforce dependency instead of ownership?

- How do we model empowerment in our coaching conversations?

- Where might fear or control be limiting our ability to empower others?

- What stories do we want people to tell about how we lead?

Do

This week, practise Empowering Others to Own Their Choices.

In your next coaching conversation or leadership challenge:

1. Listen with empathy.
2. Ask: *"What do you want to do?"*
3. Explore options without solving for them.
4. Expect action: *"What's your next step?"*
5. Encourage reflection and follow-up.

Say: *"I trust you to own this, and I'm here to support you."*

Empowering leaders raise capable people, not dependent followers.

End-of-Week Reflection

Personal Leadership Check-In:

- Where did I practise empowering leadership this week?
- Where did I notice myself rescuing or deciding for others, and why?
- How did people respond when I handed back ownership?
- What do I need to keep practising to lead a culture of powerful, responsible choices?

WEEK 36:

HEALTHY BOUNDARIES IN LEADERSHIP LONGEVITY

"Daring to set boundaries is about having the courage to love ourselves, even when we risk disappointing others."
—Brené Brown

Learn

Boundaries are essential for sustainable leadership.

Without boundaries, leaders drift into:

- Burnout
- Resentment
- Over-functioning
- Disconnection from purpose

Healthy boundaries are not walls—they are guidelines for protecting what matters most:

- Your values
- Your energy
- Your time
- Your integrity
- Your relationships

Boundaries are not about keeping people out—they are about keeping yourself whole.

Leaders with healthy boundaries model strength, clarity, and respect.

Consider

Imagine a leadership culture where boundaries are blurred or absent.

Leaders say yes to everything. Work spills into every part of life. People operate from exhaustion, not overflow.

Now imagine a leadership culture where boundaries are clear, consistent, and modelled from the top.

Expectations are known. Priorities are protected. Health is normalised. Teams thrive because leaders thrive.

Healthy leaders lead longer—and better.

Let's Make It Real

Share a story of a boundary you've set in leadership that protected your health, your family, or your values — what was the impact?

Alternatively, reflect on a time when poor boundaries led to frustration, fatigue, or relational damage.

Invite the boardroom to reflect on where boundaries need strengthening in this leadership season.

Discuss

Choose 2-3 of these for discussion.

- Where do I currently need to strengthen or reset a boundary?
- What boundaries do we model well in this leadership team, and where are they unclear?
- How would our people describe our example of healthy boundaries?
- What rhythms or habits support sustainable leadership for us?
- What is the cost of boundary-less leadership in our culture?

Do

This week, practise Healthy Boundaries.

Consider:

- Protecting time for deep work. Turn off notifications or decline unnecessary meetings.
- Setting clear limits on availability after hours.
- Saying no kindly but clearly to a request that doesn't align with your priorities.
- Resetting a boundary that has slipped or been crossed.

- Modelling respect for others' boundaries as well as your own.

Say: *"This boundary protects what matters most—for me and for us."*

Healthy boundaries sustain leadership health.

End-of-Week Reflection

Personal Leadership Check-In:

- Where did I practise healthy boundaries this week?
- Where did I notice boundary drift, and what caused it?
- How did my boundaries support my leadership effectiveness and well-being?
- What do I need to keep practising to lead with clarity, health, and sustainability?

WEEK 37:

CELEBRATING ORGANISATIONAL WINS TOGETHER

"What gets celebrated gets repeated." —Andy Stanley

Learn

Celebration is not extra—it's essential for culture.

Leaders who skip celebration create teams who feel unnoticed, unvalued, and disconnected from purpose.

Celebration reinforces:

- What matters most
- What behaviours build culture
- What success looks like here
- Who we are becoming together

Celebrating wins together is not about ego—it's about gratitude, connection, and momentum.

Great leaders celebrate:

- Small wins as well as big ones
- Progress, not just perfection
- Effort, not just outcomes
- People, not just performance

Celebration creates energy for the next challenge.

Consider

Imagine a leadership culture where wins are ignored—where the focus is always on what's next, what's missing, or what's not enough.

People disengage. Energy drops. Ownership weakens.

Now imagine a leadership culture where wins are noticed and celebrated regularly—where people feel seen, valued, and energised.

Celebration strengthens trust, engagement, and culture alignment.

What gets celebrated gets repeated.

Let's Make It Real

Share a story of a celebration moment in your leadership that shaped culture. What did it create or reinforce?

Alternatively, reflect on a time when a lack of celebration created fatigue, disengagement, or missed opportunities for connection.

Invite the boardroom to reflect on where celebration needs to increase in their current context.

Discuss

Choose 2-3 of these for discussion.

- What do we currently celebrate well in this organisation, and what do we overlook?
- How do we create space for celebrating progress, not just final results?
- What stories of culture, connection, or growth need to be told more often?
- How do we model celebration as a leadership team?
- What would shift if celebration became a daily leadership habit?

Do

This week, practise Celebration Leadership.

Choose one intentional way to celebrate a win:

- Share a story of growth or success in a meeting.
- Write a personal note of encouragement to a team member.
- Publicly thank someone for a behaviour that reinforces culture.
- Mark a milestone together, however small.

Say: *"This matters, and we are better because of it."*

Celebrating wins together multiplies connection, energy, and ownership.

End-of-Week Reflection

Personal Leadership Check-In:

- Where did I practise celebration leadership this week?
- Where did I notice missed opportunities to celebrate progress or people?
- How did celebration affect the energy and connection within my team?
- What do I need to keep practising to lead a culture of gratitude, recognition, and shared success?

WEEK 38:

ENCOURAGING GROWTH IN OTHERS—LEGACY LEADERSHIP

*"Leadership is planting trees under whose shade
you may never sit."* —Nelson Henderson

Learn

Legacy leadership is not measured by what you build, but by who you build.

The greatest leaders aren't remembered for their achievements alone—they are remembered for the people they raised.

Legacy leaders create environments where growth is normal, development is intentional, and success is shared.

Encouraging growth in others requires:

- Seeing potential before it's visible.
- Speaking life into people before they believe in themselves.
- Handing over opportunity before they feel ready.
- Celebrating progress before perfection.

Growth happens fastest in cultures where encouragement is normal, not rare.

Encouragement is not flattery—it's fuel for growth.

Consider

Imagine a leadership culture where feedback is constant, but encouragement is rare.

People feel like projects, not people. Confidence erodes. Ownership weakens.

Now imagine a culture where encouragement is woven into the leadership rhythm—where leaders notice growth, speak it out loud, and call people into more.

People feel seen, valued, and believed in, and they lead like it.

Let's Make It Real

Share a story of a time when someone encouraged your growth in a way that shaped your leadership journey. What did their belief unlock for you?

Alternatively, reflect on a moment when you encouraged someone else and saw them rise to the challenge because of your words.

Invite the boardroom to reflect on how they currently practise encouragement and legacy leadership.

Discuss

Choose 2-3 of these for discussion.

- Who encouraged me into leadership, and what did that model teach me?
- Where am I currently investing in the growth of someone else?
- What behaviours create a culture of encouragement here?
- How do we want people to describe their experience of being led by us?
- What opportunities am I holding that I need to hand over for someone else's growth?

Do

This week, practise Legacy Leadership.

Choose one intentional act of encouragement or investment in someone's growth:

- Speak to their potential, not just their performance.
- Offer an opportunity that will stretch them.
- Publicly affirm a behaviour that reinforces leadership culture.
- Ask: *"What are you learning right now, and how can I support you?"*

Encouraging growth in others multiplies leaders and builds legacy.

End-of-Week Reflection

Personal Leadership Check-In:

- Where did I practise encouragement leadership this week?

- Where did I notice hesitation to hand over opportunity, and what caused it?

- How did my encouragement impact others' growth, confidence, or engagement?

- What do I need to keep practising to lead a culture of growth, belief, and legacy leadership?

WEEK 39:

HANDLING DISAPPOINTMENT AND FAILURE IN THE BOARDROOM

"Failure is simply the opportunity to begin again, this time more intelligently." —Henry Ford

Learn

Leadership is not about avoiding failure—it's about leading through it.

Every leader will face:

- Missed goals
- Difficult outcomes
- Relational disappointments
- Strategic setbacks
- Personal mistakes

How you handle disappointment sets the tone for how your organisation handles challenge.

Healthy leaders don't blame or withdraw—they own the reality, process it well, and move forward with wisdom.

Great leadership cultures expect mistakes and setbacks, but they refuse to let failure define identity or future decisions.

Failure is feedback—not final.

Consider

Imagine a leadership culture where disappointment is buried, failure is hidden, or mistakes are punished.

People protect themselves. Innovation dies. Trust erodes.

Now imagine a leadership culture where disappointment is processed openly and wisely.

Leaders name what's real. Lessons are shared, not shamed. Responsibility is owned. The team moves forward stronger.

Handling disappointment well teaches people how to lead through pressure, conflict, and growth.

Let's Make It Real

Share a story of a failure or disappointment in your leadership. What did you learn from it, and how did it shape you?

Alternatively, reflect on a moment when a leader handled disappointment well, and what impact it had on the team or culture.

Invite the boardroom to reflect on their current posture toward failure.

Discuss

Choose 2-3 of these for discussion.

- How do we handle disappointment and failure in this leadership team?

- Where have we modelled healthy processing of setbacks, and where have we avoided it?

- What behaviours create safety for mistakes and learning in our culture?

- What failure or disappointment do I still need to process or own well?

- How do we want people to experience leadership here, even when things go wrong?

Do

This week, practise Healthy Leadership Response to Disappointment.

Consider:

- Owning a mistake or missed expectation publicly.

- Naming what went wrong in a team conversation with kindness and clarity.

- Asking for team input on what's been learned.

- Framing failure as feedback for future growth.

- Supporting someone else who is leading through disappointment.

Say: *"This didn't go as planned, but here's what we're learning, and here's where we go from here."*

Leadership maturity is forged in failure, not success.

End-of-Week Reflection

Personal Leadership Check-In:

- Where did I practise healthy leadership in disappointment this week?

- Where did I notice avoidance, blame, or defensiveness in myself or others?

- How did my response shape trust, learning, or ownership in the team?

- What do I need to keep practising to lead with courage, humility, and wisdom through failure?

WEEK 40:

CELEBRATING ORGANISATIONAL AND PERSONAL GROWTH

"Success is a journey, not a destination. The doing is often more important than the outcome." —Arthur Ashe

Learn

Leadership is a long game, and growth is worth celebrating.

Healthy leaders know that growth doesn't happen overnight, but they recognise progress every step of the way.

Celebrating growth shifts a culture from:

- Pressure to gratitude
- Perfectionism to progress
- Fear to ownership

- Exhaustion to energy

Growth looks like:

- Character development
- Increased self-awareness
- Stronger relationships
- Healthier systems
- Courageous conversations
- Powerful leadership choices

Growth isn't just about organisational results—it's about who we are becoming together.

Consider

Imagine a leadership culture where growth is invisible—unnoticed because it's expected or undervalued.

People lose energy. Wins feel small. Ownership declines.

Now imagine a culture where growth is visible, celebrated, and shared.

Leaders pause to say:

- "Look how far we've come."
- "Remember where we started."
- "I see growth in you."

This creates energy, connection, and sustained momentum.

Let's Make It Real

Share a story of growth from the organisation, your team, or your personal leadership journey over the past season.

Reflect on what it took to grow—the challenges, learning moments, and leadership decisions.

Invite the boardroom to share their reflections on personal or team growth.

Discuss

Choose 2-3 of these for discussion.

- Where have we seen the greatest growth in this leadership team or organisation?
- What behaviours or habits created this growth?
- Where have I personally grown as a leader this year?
- Who has demonstrated growth that I need to celebrate publicly?
- What do we want to keep, start, or stop doing to lead a culture of growth?

Do

This week, practise Celebrating Growth.

Choose one intentional action:

- Write or speak words of affirmation to someone who has grown significantly.

- Tell a growth story publicly––in a meeting, an email, or a personal conversation.

- Reflect privately on your own growth and what it's taught you.

- Pause as a leadership team to celebrate where you are today, not just where you're going next.

Say: *"Look how far we've come—and look who we are becoming."*

Celebrating growth multiplies joy, ownership, and future momentum.

End-of-Week Reflection

Personal Leadership Check-In:

- Where did I practise celebrating growth this week?

- Where did I notice missed opportunities to pause and recognise progress?

- How did celebration affect energy, connection, and motivation in the team?

- What do I need to keep practising to lead a culture of gratitude, growth, and joy in this next season?

BONUS TOPICS

These extra sessions are designed to build on everything your team has already learned—giving them more chances to reflect, grow, and keep building their leadership muscles. Whether it's diving deeper into responsibility, strengthening relationships, or growing in personal confidence, these sessions offer fresh challenges and meaningful conversations to keep the momentum going.

It's all about continuing the journey and giving your team members more space to grow into the powerful, respectful, and connected people they're becoming.

BONUS SESSION 1:

CHOICES AND CONSEQUENCES— LEADERSHIP INTEGRITY

"We are free to choose our paths, but we can't choose the consequences that come with them." —Sean Covey

Learn

Leadership integrity is built on the simple but powerful principle of choices and consequences.

Every choice a leader makes shapes:

- Their reputation
- Their influence
- Their organisational culture
- Their future opportunities

Leadership integrity means understanding:

- Every choice has a cost—positive or negative.
- Every action teaches people what's normal here.
- Every decision builds or breaks trust.

Powerful leaders do not blame circumstances for their choices. They take responsibility for both their actions and their impact.

Integrity says: *"I choose my actions and I own the consequences."*

This creates leadership credibility that lasts.

Consider

Imagine a leadership culture where poor choices are minimised, excused, or blamed on others.

Trust erodes. Accountability weakens. People learn that integrity is optional.

Now imagine a leadership culture where people are free to choose, but fully responsible for the outcomes of those choices.

Ownership rises. Integrity strengthens. Trust multiplies.

Choices create culture—one decision at a time.

Let's Make It Real

Share a story of a choice you made in leadership that shaped your integrity positively or negatively. What did you learn about the power of choices and consequences?

Alternatively, reflect on a moment when you witnessed a leader take responsibility for a difficult choice. What impact did it have on trust or culture?

Invite the boardroom to reflect on where integrity needs to be strengthened personally or organisationally.

Discuss

Choose 2-3 of these for discussion.

- How would our people describe the integrity of this leadership team?

- Where do we currently lead well in modelling choices and consequences?

- Where are poor choices being tolerated, and what's the cost to culture?

- What behaviours do we need to reinforce to protect leadership integrity here?

- How do we coach others to lead themselves powerfully in their choices?

Do

This week, practise Leadership Integrity.

Consider:

- Owning a choice or decision publicly and naming the why behind it.

- Addressing a behaviour that undermines culture clarity or values.
- Coaching someone on the impact of their choices with respect and clarity.
- Reflecting on a recent decision. What were the long-term consequences, and what did I learn?

Say: *"Every choice shapes culture, and I choose integrity."*

Leadership integrity builds trust that cannot be bought, only earned.

End-of-Week Reflection

Personal Leadership Check-In:

- Where did I practise leadership integrity this week?
- Where did I notice drift from responsibility or clarity and why?
- How did owning my choices impact trust, clarity, or culture?
- What do I need to keep practising to lead with consistent integrity, courage, and ownership?

BONUS SESSION 2:

SETTING PERSONAL AND ORGANISATIONAL GOALS

"A goal properly set is halfway reached." —Zig Ziglar

Learn

Leadership without goals is leadership without direction.

Goals create focus, momentum, and alignment, personally and organisationally.

Healthy leaders set goals that are:

- Clear: Everyone knows what success looks like.
- Meaningful: Connected to purpose and values.
- Measurable: Progress can be tracked.
- Stretching: They grow people beyond their comfort zone.

- Shared: Others are invited into the journey.

Great leadership cultures set goals not just for what they want to achieve, but for who they want to become.

Goals aren't just about results—they are about growth.

Consider

Imagine a leadership culture where goals are vague, disconnected, or hidden at the executive level.

People drift. Effort is scattered. Wins go unnoticed.

Now imagine a culture where goals are visible, energising, and shared.

Teams are focused. Progress is celebrated. Alignment increases. Ownership grows.

Goal clarity creates collective energy.

Let's Make It Real

Share a story of a personal or organisational goal that shaped your leadership journey. What made it powerful or memorable?

Alternatively, reflect on a time when poor goal setting created frustration or drift. What would you do differently now?

Invite the boardroom to reflect on their current practices around goal setting, personally and as a leadership team.

Discuss

Choose 2-3 of these for discussion.

- Where are our current goals clear and aligned, and where are they vague or disconnected?

- How do we ensure our goals reflect our values, not just our targets?

- What rhythms support goal visibility, progress tracking, and celebration?

- Where do I personally need to set or reset a leadership goal?

- How do we create a culture where goal setting is normal and energising?

Do

This week, practise Setting Personal and Organisational Goals.

Consider:

- Revisiting a current organisational goal. Clarify the why, the what, and the how.

- Setting a new personal leadership goal for growth in the next season.

- Asking your team: *"What does success look like for us this quarter?"*

- Sharing your goal-setting process publicly to model alignment and focus.

Say: *"This is where we're going, and this is how we'll get there together."*

Leadership clarity creates momentum.

End-of-Week Reflection

Personal Leadership Check-In:

- Where did I practise intentional goal setting this week?

- Where did I notice vagueness or drift personally or organisationally?

- How did goal clarity impact energy, focus, or ownership in the team?

- What do I need to keep practising to lead with direction, alignment, and momentum?

BONUS SESSION 3:

INCLUSION AND DIVERSITY AS STRATEGIC ADVANTAGE

"Diversity is being invited to the party; inclusion is being asked to dance." —Verna Myers

Learn

Inclusion and diversity are not compliance checkboxes—they are strategic leadership advantages.

Diverse teams:

- Think better.
- Solve problems more creatively.
- Reflect the communities they serve.
- Create cultures of belonging and trust.

Inclusion is not just about representation—it's about full participation.

Inclusive leaders:

- Seek different perspectives.
- Create safety for honest conversations.
- Listen with curiosity.
- Remove barriers to participation.
- Honour people's stories and experiences.

Diversity without inclusion creates frustration.

Inclusion without diversity limits growth.

Together, they build healthy, future-ready organisations.

Consider

Imagine a leadership culture where everyone looks, thinks, and leads the same.

Blind spots increase. Risk of irrelevance rises. Creativity shrinks.

Now imagine a leadership culture where diversity is valued and inclusion is practised.

People bring their full selves. Teams innovate. Trust deepens.

Leaders who lead diverse, inclusive teams multiply impact, not just efficiency.

Let's Make It Real

Share a story of a time when a diverse perspective shaped a better decision in your leadership journey.

Alternatively, reflect on a time when inclusion was absent, and what it cost in terms of connection, growth, or trust.

Invite the boardroom to reflect on where inclusion and diversity need greater focus or action in their context.

Discuss

Choose 2-3 of these for discussion.

- Where is diversity reflected in our leadership team, and where is it missing?
- How do we practise inclusion--beyond representation--in daily leadership behaviours?
- What blind spots might our current leadership demographic create?
- What does a culture of belonging look like in this organisation?
- How do we create spaces where every voice is heard, valued, and respected?

Do

This week, practise Inclusion and Diversity Leadership.

Consider:

- Inviting a different voice into a key conversation or decision.
- Listening intentionally to a story or perspective different from your own.
- Asking your team: *"Whose voice is missing in this conversation?"*

- Reviewing recruitment, retention, or promotion practices through a diversity lens.

Say: *"Diversity strengthens us. Inclusion connects us."*

Inclusive leadership isn't just good ethics—it's smart strategy.

End-of-Week Reflection

Personal Leadership Check-In:

- Where did I practise inclusive leadership this week?

- Where did I notice limitations in perspective, connection, or representation?

- How did inclusion and diversity impact decision-making, culture, or trust?

- What do I need to keep practising to lead a culture where everyone belongs and contributes powerfully?

BONUS SESSION 4:

NAVIGATING PEER PRESSURE IN EXECUTIVE INFLUENCE

"You are the average of the five people you spend the most time with." —Jim Rohn

Learn

Peer pressure doesn't disappear in leadership—it just looks different.

In executive spaces, peer pressure shows up as:

- Pressure to conform to unhealthy norms.
- Pressure to avoid hard conversations.
- Pressure to stay silent on values.
- Pressure to protect image over integrity.
- Pressure to "go along to get along."

Powerful leaders know:

- Influence flows both ways—you shape the room, and the room shapes you.
- Leading with integrity sometimes means standing apart from the crowd.
- Courageous leadership holds true to values, even in isolation.

Healthy executive influence means choosing connection without compromising conviction.

Consider

Imagine a leadership culture where people stay silent to avoid conflict, fit in, or protect their role.

Culture drifts. Integrity weakens. Trust erodes.

Now imagine a leadership culture where people speak truth with courage, stay connected with kindness, and lead with authenticity.

Influence is strongest when leaders hold both truth and grace.

Let's Make It Real

Share a story of a time when you felt peer pressure in leadership. How did you navigate it? What did you learn about influence and integrity?

Alternatively, reflect on a moment when someone's courage to lead differently shaped the culture for good.

Invite the boardroom to reflect on where peer pressure may be shaping decisions more than values.

Discuss

Choose 2-3 of these for discussion.

- Where do I feel most vulnerable to peer pressure in leadership right now?
- What situations in our leadership culture require more courageous influence?
- How do we lead with connection and kindness without compromising truth?
- What boundaries help me lead from integrity over image?
- What do we want to be known for in this leadership team, even when it's hard?

Do

This week, practise Courageous Influence.

Consider:

- Speaking up in a conversation where silence has become the norm.
- Clarifying your values out loud in a team setting.
- Encouraging someone else who is standing for what's right, even if unpopular.
- Asking yourself: *"Am I being shaped by values or by pressure?"*

Say: *"I lead from values, not from fear."*

Courageous leaders influence culture with grace, clarity, and consistency.

End-of-Week Reflection

Personal Leadership Check-In:

- Where did I practise courageous influence this week?

- Where did I notice peer pressure and how did I respond?

- How did my behaviour model integrity and connection to my team?

- What do I need to keep practising to lead with authenticity, courage, and cultural influence?

EQUIPPING LEADERS FOR A CULTURE OF LOVE AND CONNECTION

At Godwin Consulting, we partner with leaders like you to create environments where joy, responsibility, and authentic connection flourish. Whether you're aiming to strengthen your personal leadership skills, build cohesive executive teams, or transform organisational culture, we're here to support your journey.

Our tailored Professional Development sessions, LoSoP Coaching, and personalised One-on-One Key Leader Consultations are specifically designed to deepen your understanding and application of the LoSoP principles. These offerings will equip you and your leadership team with practical strategies, actionable insights, and ongoing support, empowering you to:

- Lead with clarity and purpose, nurturing trust and connection at every level.

- Embed a culture of joyful responsibility and genuine restoration within your organisation.

- Raise up empowered leaders who model and multiply healthy, connected relationships.

Our Culture Orientations include:

- **Healthy Relationships**: Prioritising trust, safety, and open, compassionate communication.
- **Joyful Responsibility**: Embracing accountability as a positive, growth-oriented practice.
- **Genuine Restoration**: Pursuing authentic reconciliation and rebuilding trust after conflict or mistakes.

With our expertise in behaviour education, organisational culture, and leadership coaching, you'll gain the confidence and tools necessary to nurture a thriving community within your workplace or school.

Visit our website today at www.godwinconsulting.com.au to book your next professional development session, LoSoP training, or schedule a personalised key leader consultation.

Together, let's build a culture where love, connection, and leadership thrive.

ABOUT THE AUTHOR

Bernii Godwin holds a Master's qualification in Social Work and a Graduate Certificate in Neuropsychotherapy, building on her under-graduate degree in Human Services and Criminology and Criminal Justice, with a focus on youth and family justice. She is also a certi-fied Loving on Purpose Trainer and John Maxwell Leadership Team Member.

Over the past two decades, Bernii has worked in various roles across a wide range of schools, specialising in student well-being and be-haviour. Principals frequently seek her expertise to consult on complex behaviour and well-being issues, provide one-on-one coaching or supervision to educators and well-being teams, and deliver school-wide professional development. Her greatest passion is helping schools adopt practical tools that replace fear and punishment with purposeful behaviour education, safe connections, and empowered teachers—ul-timately increasing student engagement in their academic journey.

To connect with Bernii, please visit

www.godwinconsulting.com.au

COMING SOON!

CULTURAL ARCHITECT: CREATING SUSTAINABLE CULTURES FOR LASTING IMPACT

In Cultural Architect: Creating Sustainable Cultures for Lasting Impact, school leaders are offered a revolutionary blueprint to transform their educational environments into vibrant, thriving communities. Drawing from the Sustainable Culture Model and the Behaviour Education Matrix, this book provides a practical roadmap to overcome the common challenges of fragmented, inconsistent, or unsustainable school cultures.

Bernii Godwin introduces the transformative power of the LoSoP (Loving Our Students on Purpose) philosophy, which serves as the cornerstone of this model, empowering principals and leadership teams to nurture shared values and consistent behaviour that breathe life into school communities.

Whether you're striving for stronger staff engagement, student success, or overall community cohesion, Cultural Architect delivers the tools, strategies, and insights to build cultures that not only inspire today but stand the test of time. This book is essential for those committed to leading with purpose, creating environments where both educators and students can flourish.